W9-CNM-884

31

The Quilter's Book of Design

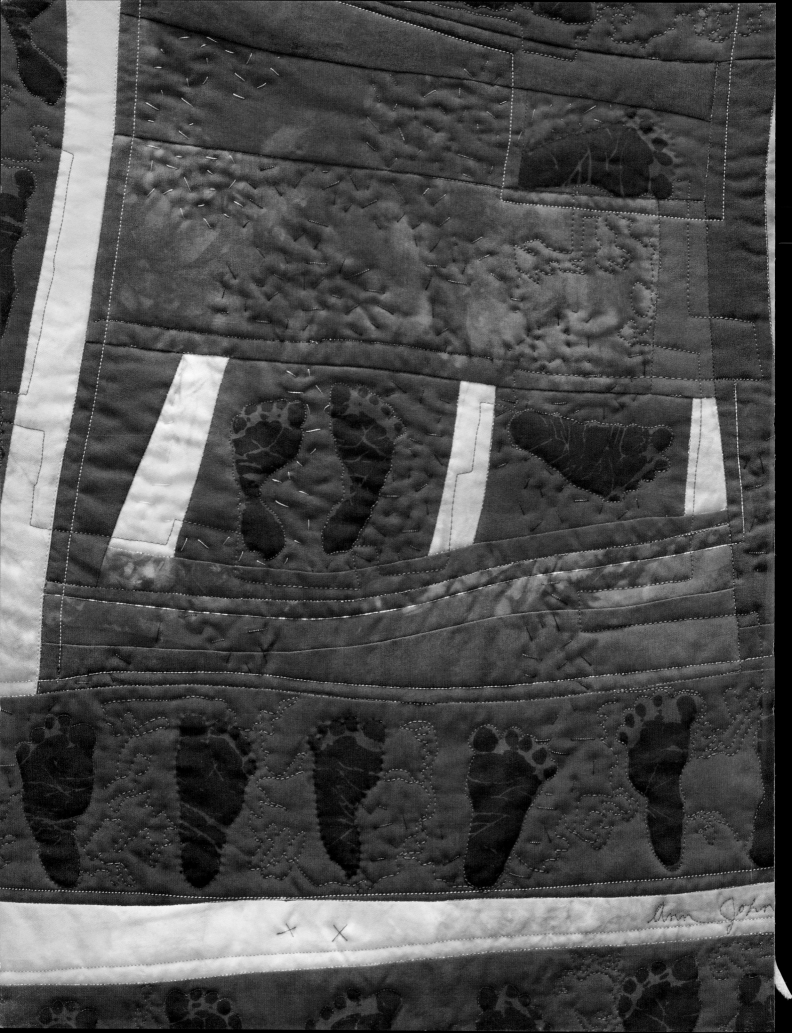

The Quilter's Book of Design

Ann Johnston

THE QUILT DIGEST PRESS

NTC/Contemporary Publishing Group

Library of Congress Cataloging-in-Publication Data

Johnston, Ann
    The quilter's book of design / Ann Johnston.
        p.   cm.
    Includes index.
    ISBN 0-8442-2660-2
    1. Quilts—Design.   I. Title.
TT835.J637   1999
746.46'041—dc21   99-25210
                             CIP

TO MY PARENTS, EDWARD AND MARION DOHERTY,

AND TO MY BROTHER, FRED DOHERTY

All the fabric in *The Quilter's Book of Design* is hand dyed by the author. The techniques she uses are thoroughly explained in her two books about dyeing fabric: *Dye Painting!*, 1992, and *Color by Accident*, 1997.

Editorial and production direction by Anne Knudsen
Art direction by Kim Bartko
Project editing by Nicole Adams
Book design by Hespenheide Design
Photography by Bill Bachhuber, unless otherwise credited
Manufacturing direction by Pat Martin

Published by The Quilt Digest Press
A division of NTC/Contemporary Publishing Group, Inc.
4255 West Touhy Avenue, Lincolnwood (Chicago), Illinois 60646-1975 U.S.A.
Copyright © 2000 by Ann Johnston
All rights reserved. No part of this book may be reproduced, stored in a retrieval system, or transmitted in any form or by any means, electronic, mechanical, photocopying, recording, or otherwise, without the prior written permission of NTC/Contemporary Publishing Group, Inc.
Printed in Hong Kong
International Standard Book Number: 0-8442-2660-2
00 01 02 03 04 05 WKT 18 17 16 15 14 13 12 11 10 9 8 7 6 5 4 3 2 1

Contents

PART 1

Design Principles

CHAPTER 1
BALANCE

CHAPTER 2
UNITY

CHAPTER 3
VARIETY

PART 2

Design Elements

PART 3

Making Design Decisions

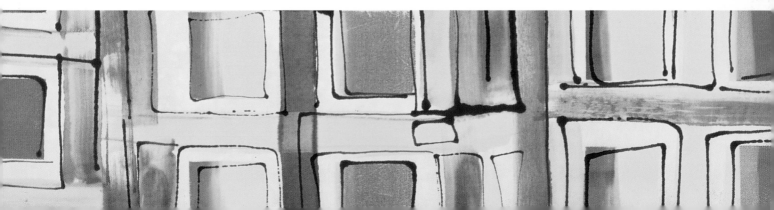

❖ ❖ ❖

Preface

As I write this preface, after the quilts, the writing, and the photography are all done, I am wondering why I took on a project like this. It has been such a long process that my plan for the book, like each of my quilts, has evolved in the making. *The Quilter's Book of Design* is twice as long as I originally intended, it took twice as long as I thought it would, and it was twice as hard to do. I think that I must have wanted to do it because I knew it would be good for me, that I would learn a lot. I was right: I learned at least twice as much as I thought I would.

Although the plan for *The Quilter's Book of Design* changed over time, the goals for the book have remained constant. I want to involve readers in basic design concepts by looking at a variety of approaches shown in my work. I want to build reader confidence in making design decisions by sharing some of my design choices. I also want to encourage quilters to start exploring for themselves by offering ideas and techniques to use as starting places.

There are as many sources of inspiration and as many ways to approach design as there are people. I think that understanding the principles and elements of design will help direct your practice and experience toward designs that better allow you to explore your ideas. Whether for quilts or for any other kind of art, understanding the functions and relationships of the elements in a design will give you more choices as you work. The knowledge will help you ask and answer questions like these: How do I emphasize or deemphasize part of the design? How do I give it more or less movement? How do I set or change the mood of the design? I hope that you will take with you the excitement of discovering some of the many possible answers in your own work.

Ann Johnston

❖❖❖

Acknowledgments

The Quilter's Book of Design would not have been written or finished without the help of these people. Anne Knudsen encouraged me to write about designing quilts and patiently waited for it to happen. Helen Grigg rescued me by sewing all those demanding traditional blocks. Sonja S. Lovas put together most of the other sample blocks and helped with every task I could dream up. Without her speed, precision, and versatility, I would still be sewing for *The Quilter's Book of Design*. Bill Bachhuber's expertise with quilt photography has given this book an added level of quality. I want to thank him for his skill and humor, and the noodle soup that made the hard work seem easier. And at the end, when I needed expert advice, Emily L. Young's thorough and multiple readings of the manuscript helped make the book clear and accurate. Without her guidance I would still be trying to decide what vocabulary to use. Meanwhile, my husband, Jim, and my sons, Scott and Tod, have kept my life lively and in perspective. I can never thank them enough.

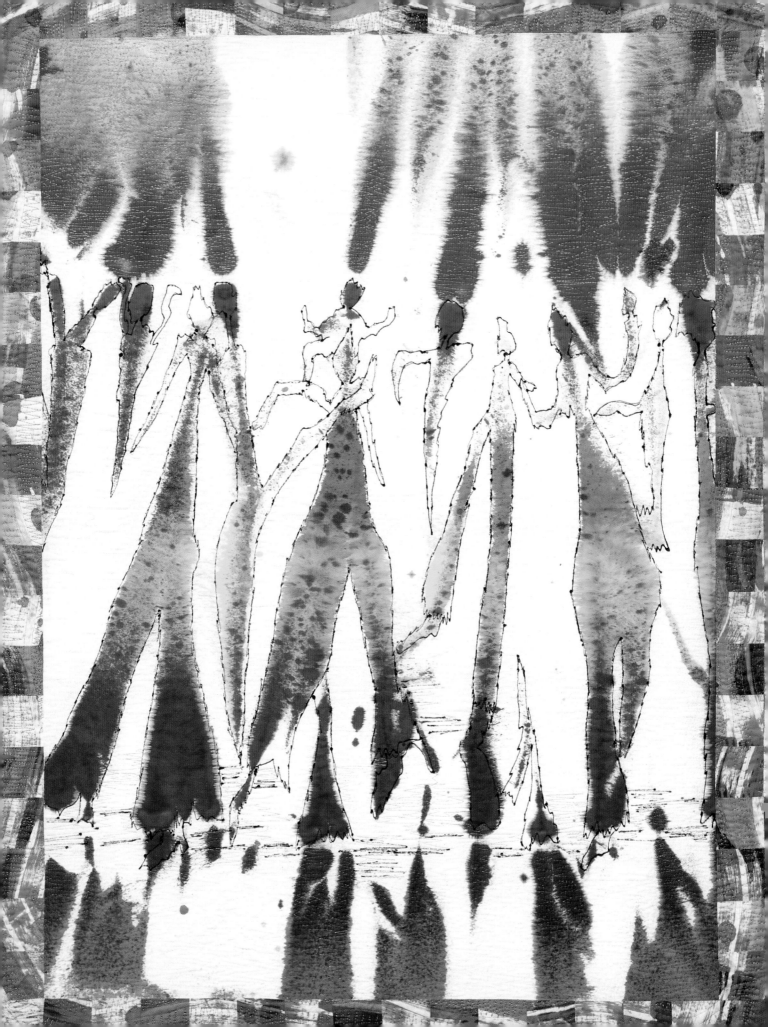

The Quilter's
Book *of* Design

PART 1

Design
Principles

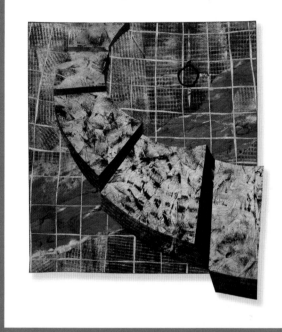

North Is Up 75" × 65", 1997.

Balancing Act I 24" × 16" 1995.

B

1

❖ ❖ ❖

Balance

Generally, people tend to seek balance in life, in nature, and in art. Balance is comfortable and imbalance tends to be uncomfortable. If we lean too far back in a chair, we are in a great hurry to get our balance back. A tipped picture on a wall catches our attention and makes us want to straighten it. Balance in a design is not as straightforward to judge as the *physical balance* we see in the world around us. It is easy to see whether a seesaw is or is not in balance, but judging whether or not a quilt design has balance is more difficult, because it is a question of *visual balance*.

Fallen Arches The yellow
shapes are larger and closer
together at the top, so the
visual weight of the design is
at the top.

VISUAL WEIGHT

In a quilt context, the word *balance* is used to describe the distribution of visual weight in a design. *Visual weight* refers to the parts of the design that appear larger, that appear to come forward, or that appear to have more importance. The elements that attract the eye of the viewer and give emphasis change the balance of a design. Some examples are size, placement, color, and texture. They are the elements that determine the type of balance a design has and how it will affect the viewer. Experience is an excellent teacher, and practice can help develop an ability to sense the type of balance in a quilt design.

HORIZONTAL AND VERTICAL BALANCE

When we look at a design, we often unconsciously assume that there is a centerline down the middle and sense the balance to the right and left of that centerline. In doing so, we are looking at *horizontal balance*. There is also a *vertical balance* to each composition: the visual weight above and below an assumed line across the middle of the composition. *New Persian* has both vertical and horizontal balance, even though the elements are not identical on both sides or from top to bottom. The center top area does not match the corresponding area at the bottom of the quilt, and the figures in the center diamond are each different colors. Even though the colors in the small triangles vary widely throughout the quilt, they all fit in the same general pattern and are balanced horizontally and vertically by the light and dark shapes.

We tend to expect to find the visual weight in the lower part of a composition, because we live with the solid

New Persian 118″ × 99″, 1996. Quilted by the
Oswego Quilters. This design has both vertical
and horizontal balance in the light and dark
shapes, even though elements are not identical
on both sides or from top to bottom.

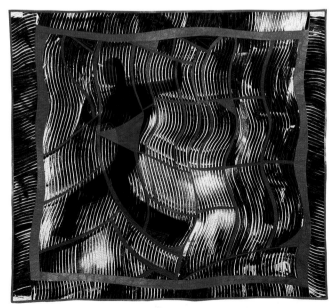

Shock Waves 41″ × 46″, 1996. The figure at left
creates unequal balance and is part of the idea of
the quilt.

Myers Quilt 100″ × 105″, 1992. An example of formal or symmetrical balance; the design is the same on both halves of the quilt, as well as on the top and bottom.

Kelp Forest 49″ × 42″, 1994. The formal structure of the blocks, and the traditional set with sashing and borders, contains the complexity of colors and contrasts with curved piecing and irregular quilting stitches.

earth below us and the light air above us. The quilt designer can plan to maintain this expectation, or to disrupt it to get corresponding results. In the unfinished quilt *Fallen Arches*, the yellow shapes are larger and closer together at the top, so the visual weight of the design is at the top. It is somewhat unexpected and so might put the viewer a little off balance. This may be the goal of the quilt, as it was when I pieced *Shock Waves*. I put the visual weight of the figure on the left side; the right side is empty except for waves: the imbalance contributes to the content of the quilt.

FOUR KINDS OF BALANCE

There are four kinds of balance, that is, four general ways to distribute the elements of a design. *Formal balance*, also referred to as *symmetrical balance*, repeats similar shapes, colors, values, lines, or other elements on both halves of the composition. This way of creating balance can give the feeling of calmness, clarity, rigidity, or rationality. *Myers Quilt* is a good example of formal balance, with an identical design on both halves of the quilt, as well as at top and bottom. Formal balance is frequently seen in traditional quilts based on blocks in a grid. *Stepping Stones*, a block used throughout this book, is a good example. Other examples are old favorites, *Nine Patch*, *Irish Chain*, *Log Cabin*, *Jacob's Ladder*, and *Drunkard's Path*.

The formality of a grid can be used to lend some organization to a complex or busy image. The grid of straight-line sashing in *Kelp Forest* allows the eye to follow a pattern and take in all the complexity of curves and color behind it. The

Stepping Stones This traditional block design has formal radial balance. Formal balance is frequently seen in traditional quilts that are based on blocks in a grid.

6

Guatemala This fabric design has informal balance to a high degree: the elements are not repeated on both sides of the middle.

Leopard Lily 33″ × 40″, 1987. The visual weight is mostly in the middle; the informal balance is subtle, at first giving the impression that both sides are similar.

BAQ, 93 7½″ × 7½″, 1993. The wreath blocks in this quilt have radial balance, and the quilt design as a whole radiates from the center.

formal border contains the design and contrasts with this complexity in the center of the quilt. This is a quilt with formal balance amid the chaos of its color.

Informal or *asymmetrical balance* uses dissimilar shapes with unequal visual weight to attract the eye. It can convey a casual, natural, or unplanned feeling. However, it is more difficult to plan informal balance because there are more decisions to make. It is harder to decide what is balanced when you are looking at different shapes, lines, colors, or other elements on each side of the design. Informal balance can be subtle, as in *Leopard Lily*, where the visual weight is mostly in the center and the impression is that both sides are similar. Informal balance can be more extreme, as shown by the design Guatemala. The elements are not repeated on both sides of the middle. Even though both sides are very different, the asymmetrical composition still gives the feeling of balance.

Circular or *radial balance* occurs when all the elements radiate from a central point in the design. The point from which the elements radiate may be in the center of the composition, in which case the design has formal balance, or the elements may radiate from a point off center, making the composition more informal. Many traditional quilt block patterns are radial. All the shapes in the *Stepping Stones* block radiate from a center point. A medallion setting for a quilt uses the principle of radial balance. In *BAQ, 93*, not only are many of the individual blocks designed with radial balance, but the center placement of the large wreath and the direction of the remaining blocks and the border all make this a composition based on circular or radial balance. *Dancing Horses*, although not a traditional quilt pattern, is based on the traditional center medallion placement with formal, vertically symmetrical borders.

Allover patterns without a focal point also have a kind of balance called *crystallographic balance*. The balance comes from having equal emphasis over a whole composition, as in *Welcome to the Zoo 2*. The primary colors are of equal intensity and are spread more or less evenly over the whole. I would like to do this one over and over, seeing what would happen to the design, for example, by putting colors in stripes, by using different values of the colors graded from top to bottom, by using color in the background only. Most designs made for fabric use allover patterns for the obvious reason that the fabric will have many different uses and the elements will be placed in many ways. Many quilts use crystallographic balance in a grid. The

Dancing Horses 37" × 30", 1987. Hand quilted by Dorothy Campbell. Although not a traditional quilt, *Dancing Horses* has formal, radial balance and symmetrical borders.

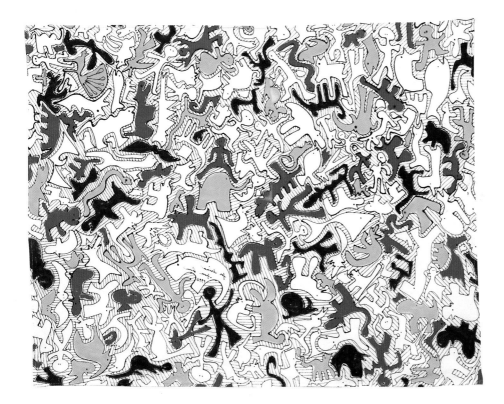

Welcome to the Zoo 2 42" × 56", flannel blanket, 1996. Allover patterns without a focal point also have a kind of balance called *crystallographic balance*, achieved by having equal emphasis over the whole composition.

Leaves 2 48″ × 48″, 1995. The leaf shapes are
of approximately equal visual weight and give
the impression of being spread all over the
quilt, an example of crystallographic balance.

Plaid Blockwork 60″ × 46″, 1989. Hand
quilted by Linda Nolan. The block setting
traditionally used in quilts lends itself to
overall design balance.

block setting traditionally used for quilts lends itself to overall design balance, as seen in *Plaid Blockwork*. *Leaves 2* also has crystallographic balance without a grid. The leaf shapes are not exactly the same from side to side or from top to bottom, but they are of approximately equal visual weight and give the impression of being spread all over the quilt.

Formal balance is straightforward and easy to plan. In quilts, it is seen frequently in traditional block patterns and settings. Formal balance can be easily applied to nontraditional designs and piecing as well, but the big puzzle is informal balance. If you want the casual or natural balance that is more like our everyday physical world, it takes much more experience to judge what dissimilar elements will balance each other. This experience comes from practice.

Experiment with your quilt designs; change your arrangement of the elements, such as the lines, shapes, and colors, as many times as possible, and step back to view its balance. Understanding some basic principles that apply to balance may help you when you are experimenting.

HOW TO CHANGE BALANCE

Variety and contrast draw our attention. The contrast of shape, color, value, texture, position, and line direction can be used to create more visual weight. For example, a complex shape, even though smaller, has a stronger attraction to the eye of the viewer. Complexity of shape, as in *Checked Triangle*, can balance a much larger simple shape of the same value and color. The irregularity of the shape on the left side of the design is different enough from the two smooth triangles on the right to create an asymmetrical balance.

A sharp contrast in color can give a small object more significance in a large space. The color might be warm in a cool composition or bright on a neutral background. The intense color of the small triangle at left in *Deep Magenta* attracts our eye at least as much as the two duller-colored triangles at right. The value of a color can also emphasize an area of a composition and make a smaller area balance a larger one in a design. The dark shapes grouped together at left in the *Dark Curtain* block seem to have as much visual weight as all the rest of the light shapes. An area of complex pattern or texture can balance a much larger area with less visual interest, as in *Dotted Triangle*.

The placement of shapes is important in the visual balance of a design. Ambiguous placement—for example, near an edge of the design—can balance another large element. The two small triangles at the top of the block *Two on the Edge* outweigh the much larger triangle placed at lower center. The direction of the lines, either implied lines or actual lines, can add visual weight or importance to an area of a design, creating a kind of balance, even though elements in other parts of the design may be larger, brighter, or more complex. In *Flag Lines* there are more large triangles on the right half of the design, but the line direction moves toward the left edge and gives it more visual weight than it would have without the influence of line direction.

Checked Triangle The complexity of the triangle at left in the design is different enough from the two smooth triangles to balance them visually.

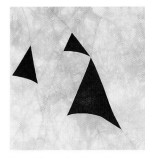

Deep Magenta A smaller area with greater color intensity can balance a larger shape in a design because it attracts the viewer's eye.

Dark Curtain The dark shapes grouped on the left side of the block seem to have as much visual weight as all the light shapes.

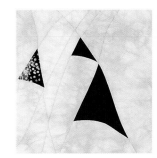

Dotted Triangle An area of complex pattern or texture can balance a much larger area with less visual interest.

Two on the Edge The two small triangles at the top of the block visually outweigh the much larger triangle placed at lower center because they are near the edge.

Flag Lines The direction of the lines at left in this block balances the greater size and number of triangles on the right side; the pattern at left has more visual weight than it would without the influence of line direction.

WE LOOK FOR BALANCE

We look for balance everywhere. I was picking up fabric scraps one day when a few narrow pieces of variegated light purple fabric caught my eye. I started playing with the scraps and, in a few minutes, I had put together several strips with some charcoal-colored fabric. It was immediately obvious how these simple lines could create endless designs, and I tried quite a few variations before sewing it up. When I finished *Balancing Act I* (see page 2), I wanted to try more designs with those lines and play with the concept of balance.

Balancing Act I was an exercise in two colors. For the next quilt in the series, I wanted to add more elements. In *Balancing Act II*, I used more colors, a large scale pattern, and a variety of textures to complicate the balancing problem. The quilt became a construction about the balancing act of motherhood. The baby footprints and the bright gold pieced lines seem to balance each other visually. The texture and variety added by the quilting and shiny threads create the over-

Balancing Act II 40″ × 38″, 1995. Bright gold lines create a structure that balances precariously with the patterns and textures in the quilt.

Balancing Act III 57" × 55", 1996. The strong dark lines of the foreground structure balance the complexity of the lines and colors in the background.

all effect of a structure that has a lot happening in it, but one that looks like it will remain standing. The larger size of *Balancing Act III* made the planning and sewing more complex. The black lines came to be more and more like a structure as I built it piece by piece. The construction techniques became second nature by the time I finished these three quilts and have been very useful in several later quilts. As I worked on this series, I felt like a builder with a choice at every step. Which way to go, which choice will work? What step to take and still keep my balance?

Practice

1. Look at a quilt photo or one of your own quilts. Draw an imaginary line down the middle of the quilt. What kind of balance does it have? Formal or informal? Radial or allover? Which shapes, lines, colors, values of colors, patterns, or textures do the balancing? How?
2. Find an example of radial balance in a quilt magazine or book. Do you ever work with circular balance?
3. Study a quilt you like in a photograph or show. What element of the quilt has the most visible weight? Does that element have anything to do with what the quilt is about? How?

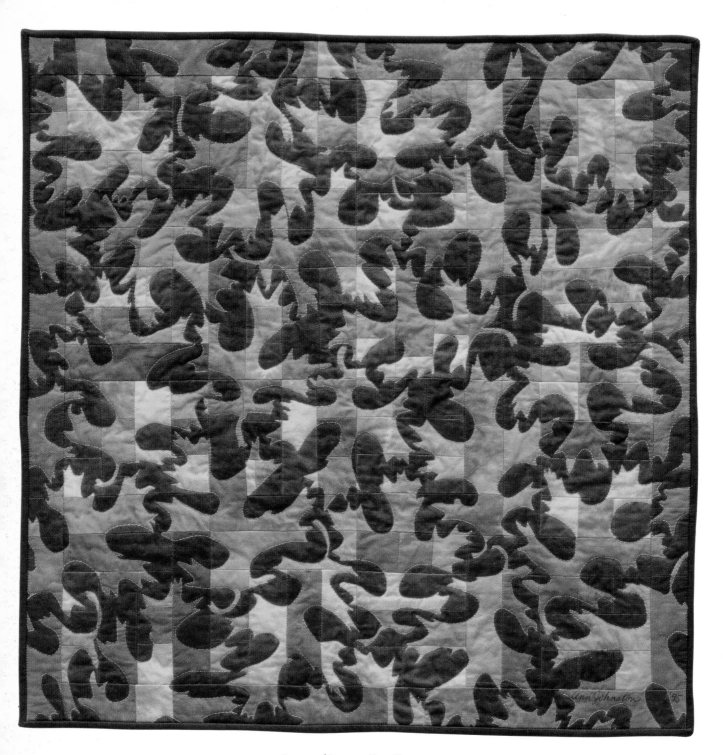

Frogs and Leaves 18" × 18", 1995.

2

❖ ❖ ❖

Unity

Another quality that we look for in visual art is unity; we look for a design that ties the elements of a composition together. The strength of a composition is that the parts are not there by chance, but that they appear to belong together. The parts don't have to be the same or have to touch each other; rather, they must make sense together. Elements in a design, like words in a sentence, can be combined in many ways, but those that are chosen have to be arranged so that their relationships enhance the visual unity, and thus the meaning of the whole composition. The challenge for the quilt designer is to make design decisions that create the intended meaning. Unity of design is achieved by the arrangement of the lines, shapes, colors, values, textures, and patterns that are used.

UNITY THROUGH PROXIMITY

One of the easiest ways to tie elements of a design together is to place them close to each other. We naturally group individual elements into larger units, trying to make sense out of them. Different shapes can be arranged in a way that gives them no unity, as in *Two Shapes*, or they can be placed near each other in a variety of ways that provide unity and may suggest a meaning. The same two shapes are used in *Column* and *Candle*, but their proximity to each other suggests a new shape in each arrangement.

When elements of a design have a similar shape, we automatically create a visual relationship among them. In the *Stepping Stones* block, the small squares create a diagonal line, but they have more relationship than just three in a row: they also suggest two lines that cross in the middle. The shapes don't even have to be touching to create a visual line. If they are similar and close together, the eye creates the line. If the small rectangles in *Two Lines* were farther apart, the suggested line would start to disappear and look like *Two Groups*.

Two Shapes These shapes seem to have no relationship to each other because of their placement.

Column The proximity of the two shapes to each other suggests one shape.

Candle The proximity of the same two shapes suggests another shape.

Stepping Stones The small squares appear to form two diagonal lines that cross in the middle.

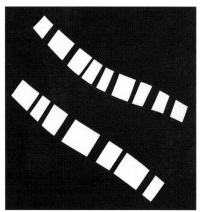

Two Lines Similar shapes, placed close together, create a visual line.

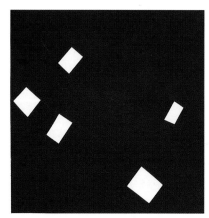

Two Groups When the spaces between similar shapes are too large, the visual *line* is lost; in this block, their proximity forms groups.

Our eyes also organize the empty spaces in a design. The foreground or positive shapes are surrounded by background, also called *negative space*. Sometimes the negative spaces compete for importance with the positive shapes. The four black shapes in *Crossroads* seem to come together to make a white line out of the background. Sometimes the background isn't as easy to organize visually and so the negative space has less definition as a shape, as in *Four Kites*. In any case, the artist has to be aware that the shapes in the foreground create shapes in the background that can confuse the viewer, or dominate the positive shapes. Traditional pieced quilts often use this principle to add complexity to a design, and with the simple change of a color or value, the same shape can become the main element of a design or it can become part of the background. It depends upon how you look at the block *Stepping Stones* whether the foreground is the white shapes or the black shapes. In the quilt top *Stepping Stones Repeated* (see page 16), the black shapes seem to dominate as foreground because they link together to create a pattern more than the white does.

Crossroads Our eyes naturally try to organize the background (white) into shapes or lines.

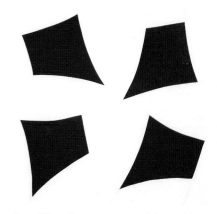

Four Kites The arrangement of the positive shapes (foreground in black) makes the negative shapes (background in white) more difficult to organize visually.

UNITY THROUGH REPETITION

Repetition is another way to create unity in a quilt design. The repetition of an element in a composition can tie the whole together, creating a relationship among the elements. In fact, repetition of an element creates *visual rhythm*, encouraging the viewer's eye to move from one element to another. The element may be a shape, a line, a color, a color value, a texture, or a pattern. It might be a straightforward repetition of the same element, or it might be a more complex composition in which the repetition is suggested, but the elements are not identical.

Static rhythm has no variety and can be monotonous if carried throughout a composition. Many traditional quilts repeat the exact same block, as in *Blue and Yellow*. If there is no variety in the fabrics chosen, the quilt will have static rhythm, that is, no movement. The Speckled Rainbow fabric has a pattern of shapes with similar color values and with similar spaces between them. In spite of the variety in each individual shape, the design has little movement.

Even using only two colors, *Stepping Stones Repeated* shows more movement and rhythm because each block has a

Blue and Yellow This quilt design has a static rhythm that might be changed completely by adding different colors or values.

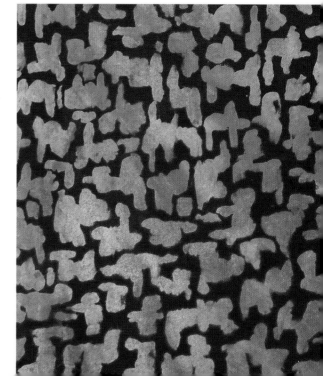

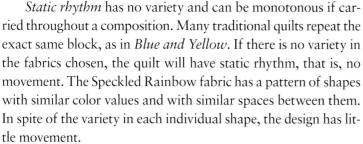

Speckled Rainbow This pattern of shapes—with similar color values and similar spaces between them—has little movement, in spite of the variety in each individual shape.

Stepping Stones Repeated Although the same block is repeated exactly, the variety of shapes *within* the block link visually, giving this design movement.

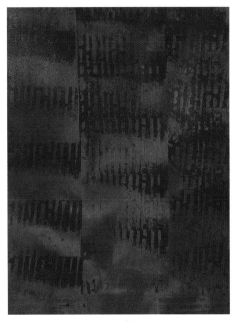

Red and Blue The colors in this fabric alternate from warm to cool, light to dark, and the visual texture appears and disappears, creating an alternating rhythm.

variety of shapes within it. The squares visually link to the squares in the other blocks, creating a different pattern than that created by the darts and the triangles. Each shape has a different rhythm in the whole composition, and the viewer's eye moves over the various patterns.

Alternating rhythm uses patterns that move back and forth. After viewing part of the design, the viewer can anticipate the element that will come next. There are many rhythms that alternate in everyday experience: light and dark, thick and thin, hot and cold, tall and short. These opposites are used frequently as rhythmic patterns in design. In Red and Blue, the colors alternate from warm to cool, light to dark, and the texture appears and disappears. *Red River* uses alternating blue and black curved lines, light and dark, to create a rhythm for the eye to follow and expect. The texture also alternates between smooth unquilted and heavily stippled areas.

Progressive rhythm uses the repetition of an element to deliberately move the viewer's eye in a specific direction. It is a pattern in which the viewer can see a

Red River 12″ × 21″, 1995. The colors, values, and textures alternate, causing the viewer's eye to move around in this design.

sequence that is predictable. An element may get progressively smaller or darker or more distorted, for example. In *Steps 4*, the size of the pyramid shapes in each column are larger in the middle; as they move toward the top and the bottom of the quilt, they decrease in size. Although they do not decrease at the same rate in each column, the viewer anticipates the progressive change and a visual rhythm is created.

Visual rhythm can be smooth and even, or it can be abrupt and uneven, depending on the goal the quilt designer wants to achieve. The black and white curved lines in *White Curves* are much more predictable than the repetition of the white circular shapes in *White Circles*. The effect on the viewer is radically different. It is up to the quilter to use the rhythm appropriate to the content of the quilt.

Steps 4, detail The sizes of the pyramids in each column are larger in the middle; although they do not decrease at the same rate in each column, the viewer anticipates the progressive change and a visual rhythm is created.

White Circles This fabric has a less predictable, uneven rhythm.

White Curves This fabric uses a predictable, even rhythm.

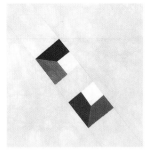

Country Block The shapes spread all over the composition in this block have no continuity.

City Block The continuity of the shared edges and the implied line give the design unity.

UNITY THROUGH CONTINUATION

A third approach to unity is the use of *continuation*, or the arrangement of various elements in the composition so that their edges create a visual line. The same pieces that are spread all over the composition in *Country Block* have continuity in *City Block* because some of the pieces share an edge. In *City Block* there are also implied lines between the shapes, created by the way they are arranged, that adds to the unity of the design.

Quilts often employ a grid as an underlying structure that gives the blocks unity through the principle of continuation. The individual block in *Blue and Rust* loses its significance when it is pieced with other similar blocks, because the lines continue through one block and the next to create a new set of shapes, as in *Blues and Rusts*. The lines between the shapes connect them and add to the unity of the composition. *Scott's Quilt* has a more complex arrangement and more colors, but the grid structure underlying it provides a needed continuity to the design.

Blue and Rust The shapes and lines in a single block are distinct and clear.

Blues and Rusts When sixteen *Blue and Rust* blocks with the same design are put together, those shapes and lines join to create completely new shapes and lines.

Scott's Quilt The underlying grid pattern gives continuity to a
complex design.

Steps 5, Lightning, **detail** The stitching matches the color of the lightning bolt in the design, using continuation of color to link the foreground to the background. The scale is similar to that of the piecing, contributing to the unity of the quilt.

Gold Leaves The lines in the background are the same color as the leaves in the foreground, tying them together.

Red Lines The background incorporates some of the same color as the lines in the foreground, tying them together.

ACHIEVING UNITY

Unity is a goal in any design, but it isn't always easy to achieve. Integrating the foreground and the background, the positive and the negative spaces, is often a problem for me. I have an image in my mind, but what do I do with all the space around it? One way to tie foreground and background together is to repeat a color in both the positive and negative spaces. The fabric Red Lines has red lines over a blue and red background. In the fabric Gold Leaves, the same color is used in the leaves, the foreground, and in the lines that continue throughout the background.

In the detail of *Steps 5, Lightning*, the background is tied to the foreground using a continuous line of gold stitching to match the color of the lightning bolt in the design. The quilting lines in *Steps 5, Lightning* are a factor in the design of the quilt because they contrast in color and value with the background fabric but match the yellow in the pieced design. The line quality of the stitches is irregular and angular, consistent with the theme of lightning. The scale of the quilting pattern is similar to that of the piecing and makes a line the viewer's eye can follow, contributing to the unity of the quilt.

Lupine 40" × 30", 1988. Hand quilted by Dorothy Campbell. The background and foreground are tied together by the texture of the hand quilting. The viewer is attracted to all the quilted texture in the background, and the whole composition becomes more unified.

In *Lupine*, the background and foreground are linked by the overlapping of the plant and the blue outline of the border; to an even greater extent, they are unified by the overall design created by the texture of hand quilting. The viewer is attracted to all the quilted texture in the background, and the whole composition becomes more unified.

Men in Lines The figures are tied together by the continuation of the diagonal lines formed by their arms and legs. If the background were a solid color, the whole wouldn't seem as unified.

The same principle also works with a patterned background. In Men in Lines, the figures are tied together by the continuation of the diagonal lines formed by their arms and legs. The whole design has greater unity because the visual texture in the background adds more continuity. If the background had been a solid color, the whole wouldn't seem as unified.

The balance of foreground and background is the choice of the quilter. I do like designs that confuse the viewer. If there is equal visual weight in the positive and negative shapes, and if they are evenly distributed, it becomes hard to tell which is which. In the case of *Salish Signs*, the balance of positive and negative space was intentional. Before I designed this coat, I studied the designs of the Native American tribes of the Pacific Northwest coastal regions. They use interlocking positive and negative spaces to create intricate, unified designs. I used this knowledge to draw the lines and shapes to fit the coat pattern I had selected. The figure and ground are so interlocked that it takes careful scrutiny to see the eagle and the whale in the lines and shapes on the coat. In the case of *Frogs and Leaves* (see page 12), I designed the whole quilt with leaf colors in

Salish Signs, **detail** Dye-painted, machine-quilted silk coat, 1993. The positive and negative areas are so interlocked in this design that it takes careful scrutiny to see the eagle's feathers and the whale's fin in the lines and shapes on the coat.

mind, quilting leaf shapes over the top of the pieced squares and rectangles; the result was practically invisible leaves. I painted dark green dye in the background behind the leaves to push the leaves to the foreground. Because the leaves are evenly spaced and about the same size as the spaces between them, the background shapes, frogs, become something as visually significant as the leaves. The fact that none of these background shapes is at all like an actual frog doesn't prevent the strong suggestion from overwhelming the whole design.

Practice

1. Look at one of your favorite traditional quilts in a book or magazine. What kind of rhythm does it have? Static, progressive, alternating?

2. Look at the quilt you are working on now. How do you plan to quilt it? Does your decision have anything to do with the design on the quilt top? Will the quilting lines have rhythm? Will they be smooth, even, and predictable, or abrupt and uneven?

3. Look for five examples of unity through proximity—that is, the visual grouping of elements—in your quilts.

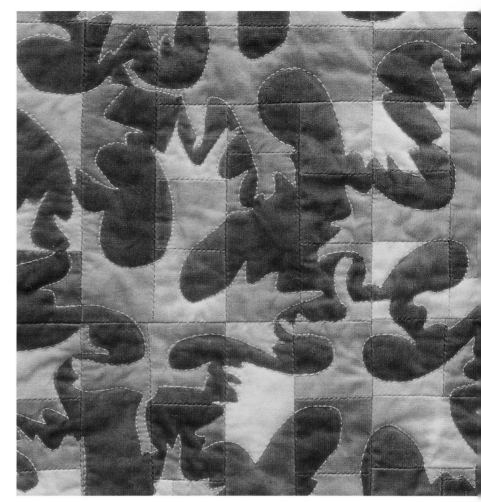

Frogs and Leaves, detail

Leaves 3 33" × 43", 1996.

3

❖ ❖ ❖

Variety

Variety is the third key to a successful design. The word *variety* refers to an element of a whole that differs from the rest in some minor characteristics. A design may satisfy a sense of balance and have a certain unity, but if it doesn't have some kind of variety or contrast, the viewer will lose interest. A successful meal is considered to need a variety of flavors that enhance each other. Nature shows us fascinating variety. Life provides us with unlimited variety. Another word for it is *diversity*. It is what makes life exciting and mysterious. Good designs must have variety, as well as unity and balance.

ariety

Diversion Even a small twist can catch your eye.

VARIETY ENHANCES UNITY

A completely uniform design can be brought to life with the tiniest bit of variation. The quiltmaker needs to decide how much variety to put into a design, to place emphasis carefully, to make it interesting but not chaotic. The black and white stripes in *Diversion* are all uniform in width and straight, except for the one that catches our eye, the one with a slight curve.

Unity should be enhanced, not destroyed, by the use of a variation. The variation can be subtle, as shown in Bricks, where the colors are all related to orange, all warm. The shapes are all similar and evenly spaced, creating a predictable pattern. Even the details within the shapes are similar. The variety can be more obvious, as shown in Dotted Lines, where the colors range from orange to its opposite, blue, from warm to cold, and the arrangement of the colors and values makes no predictable pattern. The shapes in Dotted Lines are generally rectangular, but the patterns within the rectangles vary greatly, and the spacing of the shapes changes across the fabric. Although this piece of fabric is unpredictable, having lots of variety, it is unified by its repetition of three patterns and the two main colors, gold-orange and blue-violet.

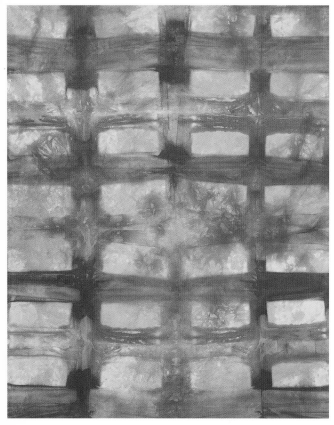

Bricks In this fabric design, the emphasis is on unity: the colors are all related to orange, all warm. The shapes are similar and evenly spaced, creating a predictable pattern.

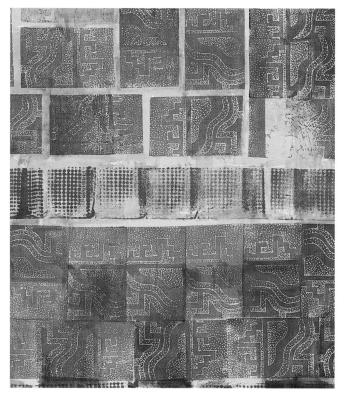

Dotted Lines Although the design in this fabric is unpredictable, having lots of variety, it is unified by the repetition of three patterns and two main colors, gold-orange and blue-violet.

VARIETY CREATES FOCAL POINTS

A problem for the quiltmaker is how to achieve both variety and unity. Just adding different elements to the composition may destroy its unity. Adding elements that are similar, but different from each other, can add interest without upsetting the unity of the whole. If one of the variations of the chosen elements is in high contrast to the rest of the piece, it can create a focal point for the composition. The focal point will attract viewers' attention, which will encourage them to look more closely at the piece. If you have a focal point, then you have used the elements in the design to emphasize a specific part of the design which should contribute to the meaning of the whole design. Adding too many focal points can actually disrupt the unity, lessen viewers' interest in a composition, or confuse viewers. Accents, or smaller focal points with less contrast to the whole composition, can be used to spread interest within it.

There are many instances of overall designs in which unity and variety are present without a focal point. The alternating rhythm of the red and black pattern in Fuchsia Checkerboard, and the variations in the colors and values of red, make a design that has unity and balance. It has variety without having a focal point. It is up to the quilter to decide if a design needs a focal point. Look at Men's and Women's. As a whole composition it might be better if it had a more definite emphasis. As a piece of fabric that will be used to make something else, it is probably better with only the vague accents of the brighter areas in the design.

Many traditional quilts were designed as overall patterns, without a focal point, and many contemporary quilts have been designed without a center to draw the eye. There really is no focal point in *Birds in Flight IV* (see page 28). How the design will be used will influence the amount and kind of variety in it.

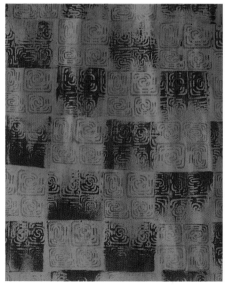

Fuchsia Checkerboard The variations in the colors and values of red make a design that has unity and balance. It has variety without having a focal point.

Men's and Women's This fabric design has vague accents in the brighter areas, but no focal point.

Birds in Flight IV 84" × 72", 1993. This quilt has an overall pattern, without a focal point to draw the eye.

WAYS TO ACHIEVE VARIETY

Change Line Direction

A change in direction of the lines or shapes in a design draws attention and adds variety. In Gold Lines, the lines are vertical on the left half and diagonal on the other. The pattern of lines is interrupted and it is the first place a viewer looks. The focal point is the place where the vertical lines meet the diagonal lines. *Leaves 3* (see page 24) uses directional change in both the shapes of the leaves and the lines of the branches and ferns. They are not all vertical or horizontal, falling or lying down, but the differences in direction are scattered across the design—not focused in one place, as they are in Gold Lines.

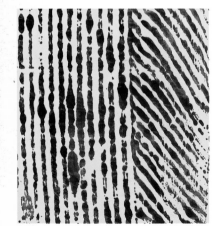

Gold Lines A change in direction of the lines or shapes in a fabric draws attention and adds variety.

Change Size

Variety in size will also draw interest if all the other elements of the composition are the same, and it isn't just the biggest that wins our attention. *Black and White Curves* has six black lines with slight variations in the shapes of their curves, but none of those variations attracts our eye as much as the narrower width of one line. It isn't the size that attracts our attention, but rather it is the difference in size from others in the same design that does so.

Black and White Curves
The contrast in size with the other lines is what attracts our attention to the narrow line in this design.

Change Color

If contrast in size is combined with a contrast in color, a focal point becomes even more obvious. The smallest element in a large composition can be the focal point if the color contrast is great enough. There is no question that the red dots are the focal point in Gray Plaid in spite of their small size. Their eye appeal, however, does not take away from the unity of the design.

Gray Plaid The contrast of color draws our eye to the small red dots in this fabric. The dots also contrast in size and shape with the other elements of the design.

The difference in hues, gray versus red, adds variety to Gray Plaid. There are other kinds of color contrasts that work to add variety and emphasis in a design. In the quilt *Balancing Act 4* (see page ii), there is strong contrast in the value of the colors, as well as a difference in the hues being used. *Balancing Act 4* also achieves variety by using colors with different temperatures. The warm gold contrasts strongly with the cool greens and cool magentas in the background.

Change Color Value

A change in the value of a color is also an excellent way to add variety to your quilt design. In *Stripes and Triangles*, the place where the color lightens and almost disappears is the place you see first and look at over and over again. The light areas in the composition group together to be a vertical line of light value in a horizontal composition. The contrast of value in *Leaves 3* (see page 24) is extreme. Most of the leaves in the upper left part are bright and light, contrasting with the dark green background, as well as with the leaves of medium and dark values. The darker leaves run diagonally across the quilt and appear in the lower corner, dividing the design into areas of light and dark, adding variety without disrupting the unity. The high value contrast of *Leaves 3* emphasizes the extreme variety of nature's autumn leaf display.

Stripes and Triangles The areas where the color lightens and almost disappears are the places we look at over and over again. The light areas in the composition group together to be a vertical line of light value in a horizontal composition.

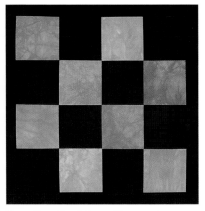

Gray-Blue The dull gray-blue stands out, even though it is not as light as the other blues, because it is not as intense.

Change Color Intensity

Dull colors and bright colors are another kind of variety or contrast to use to add interest to a design. Even a dull color will stand out if it is in a composition full of brighter colors. *Gray-Blue* is a patchwork of variations in blue on a black ground. The two lightest colors of blue-violet pop out compared to the other colors of blue, because they are lighter and warmer than the others, but the dull gray-blue also stands out. This square is not as light as the other blues, but it is different because it is not as intense. It is different and attracts attention by being duller, less saturated in color than the others.

Change Degree of Complexity

If the style of an element in a design is different from the rest of the elements, it will stand out and attract attention. For example, if one line or shape is complex and the rest of the design is made up of simple shapes and lines, then the eye will be attracted to the complexity. If the whole design is intricate and detailed, with one part that is simple and bold in style, the viewer will be attracted to the simple part. In the case of *Light and Blue I*, the eye is drawn to the small white triangles. They have high value contrast with the darker blues in the composition, but there are other white shapes that do not draw the eye in the same way. The reason the triangles are such a focal point is that they are quite different in style from the rest of the quilt: they are hard-edged and geometric, while the rest of the shapes have a hand-drawn and sketchy look. The red stripes in the quilt, one of which might have been a focal point, become only accents because there are so many of them.

Change Texture

Quilts have the extra dimension of texture that we can use to add variety, subtle or bold, to our designs. A wide variety of embellishments can add texture to a quilt, anything from the stitches that hold the layers together to beads, paint, and embroidery. Large, fancy stitches add interest to the pieced edges of some lines in *Balancing Act 4* (see page ii), adding variety without distracting the viewer. In the detail, *Leaves 3*, the quilting patterns create a variety of textures that enhance the organic subject of the quilt. The very narrow horizontal lines that change from light blue to dark blue in *Light and Blue I* are stuffed with piping. They stand out from the surface of the quilt and add emphasis to the overall horizontal quality of the design, to the calm atmosphere of the quilt.

Light and Blue I 48″ × 32″, 1989. Hand quilted by Dorothy Campbell. The small white triangles have high value contrast with the darker blues in the composition; they are also quite different in style from the rest of the quilt, attracting the viewer's eye.

Leaves 3, **detail** The quilting patterns create a variety of textures that enhance the organic subject of the quilt.

Change Placement

The placement of an element in a design can add variety and give emphasis. If one element is isolated from the others, it assumes more importance and can become a focal point. The single lemon in the upper left part of *Midnight Lemon* is emphasized more than the two lemons in the other corner because it is alone. Placement is critical. The focal point in *Four Corners* is the pale green piece near the middle of the right edge because of the combination of isolation and value contrast. The viewer's eye is led off the edge and away from the design, in this case, a serious misplacement of a piece that has such high contrast in value. If this element were placed near one of the light diagonal lines and not so close to the edge, it would not have the same effect.

Four Corners The focal point is the light green piece near the middle at the right edge because of its isolation and contrast in value with the other shapes. It leads the viewer's eye off the edge and away from the design.

Midnight Lemon 20″ × 22″, 1987. The isolation of the single lemon in the upper left part of the design emphasizes it.

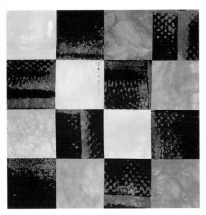

One Yellow This design has too much variety. The yellow patch is light like the blue, but it looks wrong because it focuses our attention, giving it too much emphasis.

Pink Square If an element is too different from the rest of the design, it will disrupt the unity of the design.

TOO MUCH VARIETY

Variety is achieved by using variations of the elements chosen for the quilt design, but a design can have too much variety, distracting the viewer and disrupting its unity and balance. A focal point in a composition can be the method to attract the viewer, adding variety to the composition and at the same time contributing to its unity. *One Yellow* is an example of a design that has too much variety. This pieced block uses alternating squares of light and dark. The light patches are all different colors of blue and, although the yellow patch is light, it disrupts the pattern. It looks wrong because it focuses our attention too much. Likewise, if the element is too different from the rest, if it seems not to be an integral part of the design as in *Pink Square*, it will disrupt the unity of the design. If the square were any of the colors in the design, it would work better.

In *Four Corners*, the placement of the light value piece by the edge is not the only instance of misuse of variety. Also distracting are some of the straight seams in that block. They contrast starkly with the curvilinear edges of most of the pieces; they do not have enough in common with other lines in the design, so they look out of place.

VARIETY IS ESSENTIAL

Unity can be achieved using similar shapes, lines, colors, values, patterns, and textures in a composition. Balance can be achieved by the placement of those elements according to their visual weight. It is the variety in these elements that draws us into the quilt design and moves our eyes around it and puts emphasis where the quiltmaker wants it. Variety is absolutely essential to a good design. It can be used to add a focal point to a quilt or it can be used to add accents and interest to the whole design. Variety is achieved by contrasting one element of a design with the others. *Balancing Act 4* (see page ii) uses several kinds of variety: size, value, color, placement, and direction. The contrast of value is the most significant contrast in this quilt. The light, bright golds stand out and make their own design against all the other, darker values. But adding interest and accents around the quilt are variations in the length and width of the lines, including the emphatic narrow gold quilting lines. There is a subtle variety in the shapes of the individual feet. There is variety of direction in the gold lines and in the direction of the feet. Behind the gold lines there is a great variety of shape, enhanced by the uneven edges of the quilt.

North Is Up, **detail** Some of the variety in this quilt is visible only at close range; the small patterns in the fabric, for example, and also the subtle textures and patterns created with thread.

The background fabric in the quilt *North Is Up* (see page 1) has variety in color, direction of pattern, and value, but it is tied together by its overall green hue and the repetitions of small flashes of orange-gold. It is also unified by the grid that is pieced into it, but the grid lines themselves have variety of shape. The stairs divide the background completely from top to bottom, but the river flowing diagonally under them ties these two parts together. Some of the variety in the quilt is only visible at close range: the small patterns in the fabric, for example, and the subtle textures created with thread. The quilting pattern on the stairs, shown in the detail, is noticeable only in a particular light. The design in each stair is a different scale, but has the same subject, human figures.

When is there too much variety and too little unity? The final answer about the balance of unity and variety in a composition is whether or not it works. Of course, even after you—the quilter—decide, the individual viewer makes a decision also.

Practice

1. Look at one of the first quilts you made and one of your newest quilts. Name and count the kinds of variety they each have. How do they differ? Do they have enough variety or too much?
2. Look at one of your favorite quilts in a book. Does it have a focal point? Do you use a focal point in your quilts?
3. Find an example of each of these kinds of variety in a magazine or book of quilts: size, direction, shape, value, color, texture, pattern.

PART 2

Design
Elements

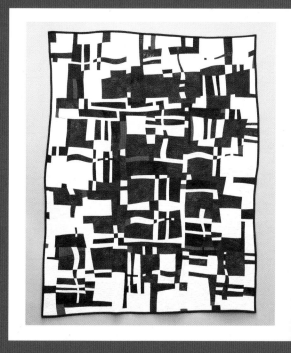

Tod's Quilt 90" × 70", 1997.

Balancing Act 7 50" × 53", 1998.

4

❖❖❖

Six Design Elements

The basic elements of a design are *line*, *shape*, *value*, *color*, *pattern*, and *texture*. They can be categorized in many ways. For the purposes of *The Quilter's Book of Design*, I want to examine these elements as tools for the quiltmaker to create a successful design: one in which balance, unity, and variety contribute to the meaning of the composition. If each element—and its relationship to other elements of the design—is understood, the quilter can make decisions about its potential to contribute to the final piece. We can use these elements intuitively or in a very academic way, but what ultimately matters is how they affect the whole design.

lements

I find it revealing to look at my quilts in terms of the elements of design. I have begun to evaluate what happens to one shape when it is put with another, or how a line was created by a contrast in color, or why my planned focal point became confused with the background. The following definitions and illustrations are meant to be an introduction to the elements of design. Succeeding chapters will elaborate on their relationships and illustrate some basic principles to learn.

LINE

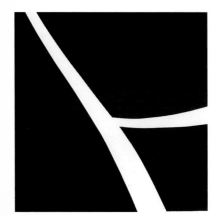

Flight A line is really a shape that has form and width, but is narrow compared to its length. One way to look at lines is to see that they create shapes and that shapes can be considered to have a line around them.

One way to define *line* is to describe it as a thin, continuous mark. It is really a shape that has form and width, but it is so narrow compared to its length that its width is not an issue. Another way to look at lines is to see that they create shapes and that shapes can be considered to have a line around them. In the pieced block *Flight*, do you see three black shapes or two white lines? The lines have shape, but the overall impact is that of a mark, a line, that flows across the block. In fact, the best thing to remember about line as a design element is that a line makes the eye follow it, it makes the eye move along its length. It is the quilter's tool to denote direction and movement.

SHAPE

A *shape* is a two-dimensional form. It is the characteristic configuration of a thing; an outline or a contour. A shape is something distinguishable from its surroundings by its outline. A shape is a visually perceived area; the edges are defined by a line or by color, value, or other changes between the shapes.

Tumble In this pieced design, there are lines between the shapes, and the shapes connect to make wide lines, but the overriding impact is that of shape.

Shapes are created by contrast with their surroundings. It helps to look at an illustration of the idea in which the composition is definitely made of shapes, not lines. In the pieced block *Tumble*, there are lines between the shapes (of course) and the shapes do form lines of a sort, but the overriding impact is that of shape. It contains several irregular shapes, with high value contrast to define them and with some similarities to unite them. In fact, the black shapes are of approximately the same size and quantity as the white shapes, so the viewer is left to decide which is the foreground and which is the background.

VALUE

Value can be defined as the degree of lightness to darkness of a color. It is the amount of light reflected to the viewer's eye. In color theory, black reflects no light and white reflects all of it. The viewer is really only concerned with how the value looks compared to the surrounding values. The same color of gray may look dark compared to one gray and light compared to another.

Value is most easily seen in a black-to-white scale: in the printed fabric Hi Tech, the various values of gray are created by the density of the black dots. The change in the relative darkness of the shapes adds interest to the design.

When there are many colors present, it is harder to judge value, but it is critical to be able to see value changes in a color composition and employ them to the advantage of the design. Two different colors with the same value in a composition can have less contrast or impact than two different values of the same color. Contrast of value is often the key to the success of a strong design.

Hi Tech In this piece of hand-printed cotton, the various values of gray are created by the density of the black dots. The change in the darkness of the shapes adds interest to the design.

COLOR

Color is what we see when light is reflected off an object. We perceive different colors, determined by the wavelengths of that light. The words *hue* and *color* are often used interchangeably, but it is more useful to use the word *hue* to mean the name of the color: that is, one of the ways we describe the color. Color also is described in terms of value (lightness and darkness) and intensity (brightness and dullness). The primary colors are red, yellow, and blue. So the color red, for example, as a very light value might be named pink and as a less-intense red, with some green in it, might be named burgundy.

The dyed fabric Color Waves has all the primary colors; where they overlap, secondary colors are produced. Where all three primary colors mix, less intense colors appear as browns and grays, which are the least saturated, the least reflective.

It is important to be able to see what color is doing in a design; we must analyze how one color contrasts or blends with another color in hue, value, and intensity, and how that affects the success of the design.

Color Waves This fabric has all the primary colors; where they overlap, secondary colors are produced. Where all three primary colors mix, browns and grays appear.

Brush Marks The white shapes and lines create several patterns on this fabric. Even a small area of dots can be perceived as a pattern if it contrasts distinctly with other parts of the design.

PATTERN

Pattern is a repetitive design with a motif appearing again and again. A pattern is created when the viewer is led to anticipate the same elements in a design. The repetition does not have to be symmetrical, nor does it have to be precisely placed for the viewer to be able to anticipate or find a pattern. Sometimes a pattern is noticed by one viewer and not another; the quiltmaker should be aware of the degree of patterning.

In the resist-dyed fabric Brush Marks, the white shapes and lines create several patterns. Even a small area of dots may be perceived as a pattern if it contrasts distinctly with other parts of the design.

TEXTURE

Texture is the surface and tactile quality of an object. In many kinds of artwork, texture can be seen where there actually is no texture to feel: for instance, a smooth-surfaced photograph can show visual texture.

In quilts, in addition to using fabrics that have marks on them that appear to be texture, the fabric itself has an actual texture. Different fabrics can be used to create a contrast in textures as part of the quilt design. In addition, quilting stitches change the actual texture of the surface, and embellishments can be used to provide an almost limitless variety of surface textures.

In order to avoid confusion, I will use the word *texture* for the presence of real surface variety; when referring to the appearance of texture, I will use the phrase *visual texture*. In *White Texture*, the surface of the block is actually bumpy and does have loose threads hanging in rows, as well as heavy ridges of satin stitching. The visual texture is there in the photograph.

White Texture Different fabrics can be used to create a contrast in the actual texture of the quilt. In addition, quilting stitches and embellishments can be used to change the surface of the quilt.

Balancing Act 5 (Ladder) 27" × 41", 1996.

5

✦ ✦ ✦

Line and Shape

Which comes first, the line or the shape? It doesn't really matter, but it is a good idea to be aware that lines define shapes, and shapes create lines. A line is a shape that is narrow compared to its length. Shapes have lines around them, whether they are drawn or just implied by the edge of the shape. When you use one, you may be creating the other. When you draw a line, notice the shape you have created; when you sew one shape to another, note the lines that are created by the contrast of the shape with the background. Are the black areas in Hi Tech (see page 39) lines or shapes? Note how the black and gray areas create white shapes in the background.

LINE

Lines may be straight or curved, delicate or bold. They may be vertical, horizontal, or diagonal. They can suggest direction, movement, mood, and emotion. Shapes and lines are used in piecing, appliqué, and quilting. The quilter should be aware that the type of shape or line determines the effect it has—smooth, jagged, bold, subtle. The flowing lines in *Flight* (see page 38) give a completely different sensation to the viewer than the jagged lines created by the shapes in *Tumble* (see page 38).

Not only in piecing, but also in embroidery (whether surface embroidery or through all the layers as quilting lines), the line quality should be a definite consideration. A curved stitching line will work better on some pieces than an angular line. The stitched line not only creates shape but also texture; the choices made can enhance or detract from the overall feeling of the quilt.

Three Kinds of Line

There are three kinds of line: an *actual line*, an *implied line*, and a *mental line*. An actual line is physically there in the design; an implied line or mental line is created visually by the elements. A composition may have all three kinds of line. The actual line is probably the most common element of design and is used everywhere in art and graphics. However, in pieced designs, it is used much less frequently. Borders and sashing are actual lines in quilts and often act to contain or define the designs within them. Some quilts, referred to as string quilts, use a bunch of lines sewed together, but the lines often do not show up as line; instead, they act to create shapes. In *Steps 5, Lightning* the blue-and-white and black strips make blocks. Where the color contrast is high, the strip appears to be a line. Where it is low, strips join to make a shape. The yellow strips mostly stand out as lines because of their contrast with the colors around them.

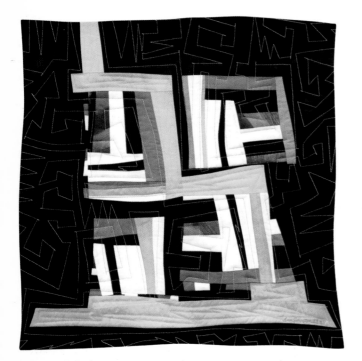

Steps 5, Lightning 19" × 19", 1995. Where the color contrast is high, strips appear to be lines. Where contrast is low, strips appear to make a shape.

Appliqué quilts often employ lines as part of the design, but in most pieced quilt blocks, geometric shapes are predominant. Those shapes may link up to create a line, as the small squares do in *Stepping Stones Repeated* (see page 16). The machine stitching lines in *Balancing Act 5 (Ladder)*, shown at the beginning of this chapter, emphasize the piecing design and the shapes in the fabric; they also add shapes and texture to the background.

A line is implied when the viewer visually connects the elements of the composition. If a quilt is constructed in blocks, it is only when all the parts are put together that the implied line will be seen. In *Kelp Forest* (see page 5), the shapes in each block visually continue across the sashing strips to become long lines. In *Scott's Square*, the block illustrates how, where the edges of the curved shapes are different in color and value, they can be seen as lines. When the curved shapes continue across dark areas where there is little contrast and the line almost disappears, the eye automatically continues the line. In an overall design like *Red Flags* (see page 54), the viewer's eye follows the curving line of the overlapping red shapes. We look for these relationships between shapes and create lines with them.

A mental line is drawn when we feel a connection between the elements of the design or when we follow a line of sight created by them. In *Merry-Go-Round 2* (see page 53), the line of sight is the direction in which all the animal figures are facing—where they are going. In the quilt top *Menagerie 6*, the mental lines move from the lower right and left corners up to the central figure. The merry-go-round characters are all looking toward or moving in that direction. In *Merry-Go-Round 2*, I meant to show the figures escaping, so the line of sight goes off the right side of the quilt. In *Menagerie 6*, I want to show the figures in their respective roles in the merry-go-round: the horses run the show, so the mental lines direct the viewer toward the large horse in the center.

Scott's Square Where the edges of the curved shapes are different in color and value, they can be seen as lines.

Menagerie 6 The mental lines move from the lower right and left corners up to the central figure in this design. The merry-go-round characters are all looking toward, or moving in, that direction.

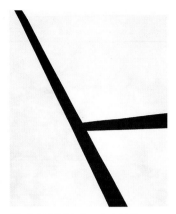

Straight Flight The straight lines give this block a rigid look.

Curved Flight The slight curve in the lines makes them seem more flowing.

Uses of Line
Use Line to Express Mood

An artist uses the element of line to make the design communicate. Line can be used to express emotion, mood, and attitude. Look at the difference in character of the two blocks with pieced lines, *Straight Flight* and *Curved Flight*. Lines can enclose, give a sense of safety, as in *Be Safe* or they can *Jolt* the viewer. Even the simplest line is expressive. Lines can dance, as in *Dancing Lines*, or be angry and confused, as in *Messed Up*.

In the quilt *Light and Blue II*, the horizontal lines contribute to the overall sense of calm. The horizontal lines of the piecing continue through the borders, and most of the quilting is horizontal. Where the quilting lines are curved in the foreground, they add subtle shapes; where the diagonal quilting lines contrast with the horizontal, they create a border effect.

Be Safe Lines can enclose and give a sense of safety.

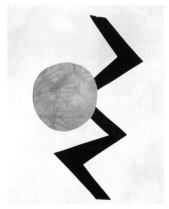

Jolt The character of the line can convey meaning to the viewer.

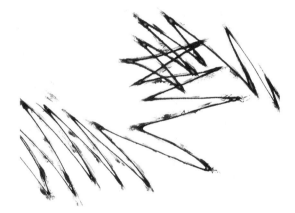

Messed Up A line can express anger or other emotions.

Dancing Lines Lines can dance, slow or fast.

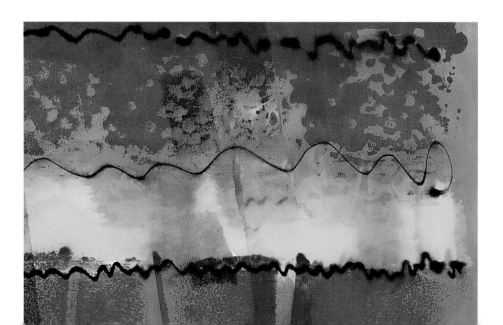

Light and Blue II 24″ × 33″, 1989. Hand quilted by Dorothy Campbell. The horizontal lines of the piecing continue through the borders, and most of the quilting is horizontal, giving it an overall sense of calm.

Use Line to Create Shapes

Lines can create shapes or outlines; even with little detail, they can be used to suggest or to symbolize real objects. Lines can build a ladder, as in the pieced block *Gold Ladder*, or they can put a bird in the sky, as in the appliqué block *Gull*.

Lines can represent people without having much to do with reality at all. The quilting lines in the detail of *North Is Up* (see page 33) suggest figures in action. The dyed lines in *Welcome to the Zoo 2* suggest animals, even though the only clue to their identity as creatures is a dot for the eye. In both quilts, the lines do double duty; they suggest figures and fill a space. In *North Is Up*, the quilting lines create an overall texture and, in *Welcome to the Zoo 2*, the painted lines create an overall pattern.

Gold Ladder Many complex objects can be represented by a combination of simple lines.

Gull A single line can symbolize many things, depending on which way it is viewed.

Welcome to the Zoo 2, detail 29″ × 31″, 1994. The lines suggest animals, even though the only clue to their identity as creatures is a dot for the eye.

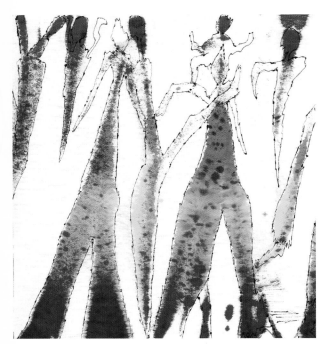

Use Line for Emphasis

Lines can be used to enhance the contours of a shape, to emphasize a direction, to suggest a figure or an idea. The black lines in *Balancing Act 5 (Ladder)* (see page 42) add a pattern which accents the light tan areas, and they also divide and give direction to the flow of the shapes. In *Birds in Flight IV* (see page 28), the black lines help make the blurry white shapes into birds by their slight suggestion of wings and bodies. The lines contribute to making the design fit the concept of birds in flight. The same is true in the detail of *Night Dancers*: without the emphasis of the lines, the figures would be less obvious.

Use Line to Direct the Eye

Lines can be used to direct the viewer's eye around the composition. In both *Far Out* and Big Brush, the lines lead your eyes around and back to start over again. In both, the width of the line affects the viewer's impressions of the importance of the line. Where it is thinner, it seems less significant and where it is wider and darker, it attracts the eye more.

Lines also suggest texture where there is none. In *New Amish Landscapes I*, the bold swirling lines of bright colors move the viewer's eye in circles, overriding the straight lines of the sashing between the blocks. The narrow line of the blue border encloses, contains, and calms the movement.

Night Dancers, **detail** Without the added emphasis of the lines, the figures would be less obvious.

Far Out The lines lead your eyes around and back to start over again. The width of the lines affects the viewer's impression of its importance.

Big Brush This printed cotton is smooth, but it shows the texture of the dye as the paintbrush applied it to the Plexiglas, and it shows the wrinkles and folds in the fabric when it was printed.

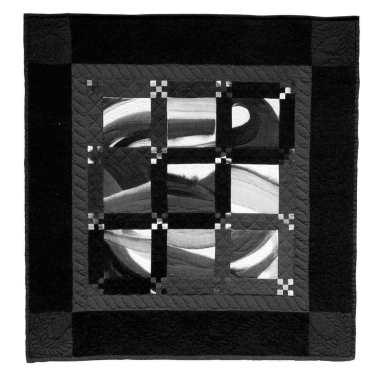

New Amish Landscapes I 44″ × 44″, 1989. The bold swirling lines of bright colors move the viewer's eye in circles, overriding the straight lines of the sashing between the blocks. The narrow line of the blue border encloses, contains, and calms the movement.

Use Line to Suggest Movement

Frequently, lines are used to express movement. The direction of a line, whether it is horizontal, vertical, or diagonal, can enhance a composition and create a particular movement. A horizontal line suggests calm, quiet, repose, like lying down. A vertical line suggests a more active or upright mood. A diagonal line creates the sensation of either up or down motion. *Quiet Lines*, *Upright Lines*, and *Moving Lines* illustrate this principle.

Motion is the primary impression made by the lines and shapes in both *Birds in Flight IV* and *Bird of Paradise*. Wings of birds in the air are often diagonal, and the flower called Bird of Paradise also has many diagonal parts that suggest a bird in motion.

Use Line to Create Depth

Lines can be used to create a sense of three-dimensional space and show distance between objects. We see the world in perspective. Linear perspective is an artist's method of creating a visual sense of depth in two-dimensional designs. It can have multiple points of view and vanishing points and may become a complex system. In the world around us, parallel lines like the edges of a highway seem to narrow and come closer together in the distance at the horizon line. By applying the basic concept of one-point perspective in which parallel lines converge in the distance, you can give a design a sense of space. The pieced block *Three Roads* has a sense of depth and suggests that there is a varying amount of distance between its horizontal lines. This impression is an illusion: there is only a flat piece of fabric and all the shapes are the same distance from the viewer.

Quiet Lines A horizontal line suggests calm, quiet, repose, like lying down.

Upright Lines A vertical line suggests a more active or upright mood.

Moving Lines A diagonal line creates the sensation of motion, either up or down.

Bird of Paradise 58" × 82", 1994. Wings of birds in the air are often diagonal, and the flower called Bird of Paradise also has many diagonal parts, suggesting a bird in motion.

Three Roads By applying the basic concept of one-point perspective, in which parallel lines converge in the distance, you can give a design a sense of space.

What the Watchman Sees 43″ × 52″, 1992. The road narrows in the distance, but the sizes of the objects on the road and around the edges of the quilt are too large for the road. This distortion of perspective is a way to give emphasis.

The viewer's expectation of perspective can be of use to the designer. In *What the Watchman Sees* I used the concept of the road narrowing in the distance, but the sizes of the objects on the road and around the edges of the quilt are too large for the road. This distortion of perspective is a way to give emphasis to the question, What is wrong here?

SHAPE

So which comes first, the line or the shape? The word *design* is often defined as the arrangement of shapes. A *shape* is a visually perceived area, and the edges are defined by a color, value, pattern, or texture contrast. The word is most often used to refer to a two-dimensional shape, that is, a flat area. Volume and mass refer to the three-dimensional shapes of sculpture and architecture. Even though quilts have dimension in the relief created by quilting and embellishment, they are usually considered two-dimensional because the angle of viewing doesn't critically change the image. The ability to see shapes in three-dimensional objects is needed to make the translation to the two-dimensional quality of a quilt.

Three Kinds of Shape

There are many ways to think about how shapes work in a composition. There are three ways to describe shapes in respect to how they look: *realistic*, *abstract*, or *nonobjective*. I painted the shapes in *Rock Garden II: Paint Brush* to show shadows and values like the granite and wildflowers that I saw in the high Sierras.

Both of my merry-go-round quilts use realistic shapes that have been idealized (see pages 45 and 53). Carousels do not use realistic pigs and frogs and rabbits, they use a more colorful version, attractive to children. No collection of animals would dance around together in a perfect circle and no pig has such rosy cheeks as those in *Menagerie 6* (see page 45). The idealized images of the merry-go-round animals fit my theme for the quilt, which is memories of childhood.

When a shape is an abstraction, it is simplified or transformed from a real object. The amount of abstraction can range from slight to extreme. The silhouettes of people in *Seaside II* are simple outlines that resemble the real objects. A transformed shape can be used to provoke a response in the viewer and to emphasize elements in the subject. *Night Dancers* gives emphasis to the dancing, rather than to the bodies, by exaggerating the legs and postures of the figures.

Rock Garden II: Paint Brush, detail A shape can be a realistic or natural representation of the actual object.

Seaside II, detail 33″ × 39″, 1987. Hand quilted by Dorothy Campbell. The amount of abstraction can range from slight to extreme. The silhouettes in this design are simple outlines that resemble real people.

Night Dancers 50″ × 36″, 1992. A transformed shape can be used to provoke a response in the viewer and to emphasize selected elements. This design gives emphasis to the dancing, rather than to the bodies, by exaggerating the legs and postures of the figures.

Bryce Canyon The elements of the design for *Vermilion Cliffs* came from this and other photos.

***Vermilion Cliffs*, detail** Simplified shapes, colors, and layers of the rocks are the basis for this abstract design. They are put together to give the same sense of balancing rocks as in Bryce Canyon.

The detail of *Vermilion Cliffs* is an abstraction of Bryce Canyon. The shapes, colors, layers, and balance of the rocks are the basis of the design for this quilt. I simplified these elements to design the quilt and to contribute to the meaning.

Nonobjective design uses pure shapes, geometric or amorphous, with no reference to any natural object. Shapes might be used to illustrate a design principle without having the distraction of realistic subject matter. Nonobjective shapes are frequently used when the subject of the work is a concept, such as the relationship of colors or an emotion. Often a viewer can see real objects in a nonobjective design. Sometimes only the title of the work lets you know. When I made *Tod's Quilt*, I was using some nonobjective shapes that I had used in previous quilts. Those earlier pieces were very complicated, but for *Tod's Quilt*, I tried to focus on simplicity. When it was all together, a viewer might be able to see all kinds of things in it, such as buildings, a city road map, stairs, or chairs (see page 35). I am not at all sure that there is such a thing as nonobjective, but certainly some shapes are less like a real thing than others. Since quilts use shape predominately, the type of shapes you decide to use are important to the composition.

The Properties of Shape
Size
Scale the shapes you choose to enhance the meaning of your quilt design. Size alone can give emphasis to a shape in a design. It can create a focal point, as in *Black and White Curves* (see page 29) where the narrowest shape is emphasized because of its difference. A large shape will appear to be in front of smaller shapes, as in *Reflected Triangles*. In the quilt *Merry-Go-Round 2*, the largest horse is emphasized by its dominant size. When I made this quilt, I printed the white horse in four sizes before it was large enough to convey the message of escape from the merry-go-round that I wanted it to achieve.

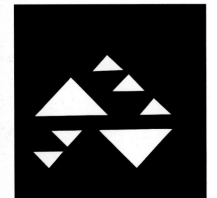

Reflected Triangles A large shape will usually appear to be in front of smaller shapes.

Proportion

Another size consideration is proportion, or the size of a shape in relationship to other shapes in the same design. Making two horses much larger and out of proportion to the other figures is unexpected and adds significance to their position in the design. Scale and proportion should have the desired effect in the composition. If the scale of a shape is exaggerated by the artist, it may command attention, make an object seem closer, or confuse the viewer, depending on how it is done. Any of these may be the desired result.

Merry-Go-Round 2 57" × 71", 1996. The two horses are out of proportion to the other animals and the white horse is the focal point by demand of its size and central location. © Canon Inc.

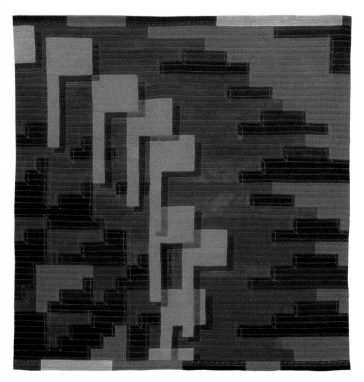

Red Flags 43" × 43", 1994. The effect of depth is greatest when both scale change and overlapping are used. If the flags changed size, the appearance of depth would increase.

Placement

Use placement of shapes for three-dimensional effects in a design. If shapes are overlapped, one appears to be in front of the other, giving a sense of depth. The red shapes in *Red Flags* not only appear to be floating in front of each other, but they also appear to be in front of the blue background and the black shapes. The effect of depth is greatest when both scale change and overlapping are used. If the flags changed size, the appearance of depth would increase.

Vertical location of shapes can also enhance the appearance of depth. An object higher in a design usually gives the impression of being farther away. That's how it looks in the real world. This principle can even take precedence over the size of an object. Even though the figures in *Key Lock Triangles* are the same size, the one on the left—that is, *lower* in the composition—appears to be closer. Unless there are signals otherwise, we automatically view the bottom of a composition as the foreground and the top of a composition as the background, farther away. The mountains in *What the Watchman Sees* (see page 50) look farther away only because they are high in the composition. In the abstract design *Strips*, the viewer may make the same assumption. The lower gold figure might appear to be closer to the viewer.

The size of a shape being smaller in the distance relates to the rule of linear perspective: as parallel lines recede into the distance, they seem to converge, and objects appear smaller than if they were closer to the viewer. That is the reason that the shapes in the lower left portion of the block *Flying Triangles* appear to be closer than those in the center top area of the block. I made the cars progressively smaller from bottom to top, low to high, and from left to right in *What the Watchman Sees* to meet this expectation.

The placement of one shape—a positive figure or foreground—creates another shape, a negative figure or background. The placement of a shape organizes the empty space around it into more shapes. The black line making each triangular shape in *Key Lock Triangles* creates a definite white shape in the middle, but the large white area around the figures doesn't seem like a shape. If the amount of figure is approximately the same as the amount of background, the effect is more pronounced and the viewer can be forced to focus on both parts of the design. For example, which do you see first, the frogs or the leaves, in *Frogs and Leaves* (see page 12)? Sometimes the effect is desired and sometimes not, but

Flying Triangles The rule of linear perspective suggests that objects appear smaller than they would if they were closer to the viewer. The shapes in the lower left portion of this design appear to be closer than those in the center top area.

Strips Elements that are higher in a design usually look farther away. In this abstract, the lower gold figure appears to be closer to the viewer.

you need to be aware of the placement of foreground/background and the possibility of the viewer seeing the background as the important shape and your foreground shape as background!

LINE AND SHAPE WORK TOGETHER

Analyzing quilts I have already made, I can see where I used painted lines in *Leopard Lily* (see page 6) and *Dancing Horses* (see page 7). I can see where I used triangles in *New Persian* (see page 4) and curved shapes in *Kelp Forest* (see page 5) to create lines. I used embroidered lines and quilted lines, lines made with piping, and lines made with appliqué, but rarely did I create lines with piecing. Only recently have I begun to cut pieces of fabric to sew into a block that are skinny enough to be considered lines and to look like lines when the quilt is finished. In *Red River* (see page 16), the lines create the design and help the viewer's eyes move around the quilt, working with the theme of the piece.

Key Lock Triangles Unless there are elements to suggest otherwise, we automatically view the bottom of a composition as the foreground and the top of a composition as the background.

Whether the line is pieced, appliquéd, painted, or quilted, be aware that it communicates something to the viewer. The lines you use create shapes and the shapes create lines. They can express connections, directions, mood, and movement. Lines and shapes can give a sense of depth to a design; they can put emphasis in a certain part of the design; and they can represent objects and ideas. You have lines in your work: decide if you want them there; determine their character; make them work for your design. If you use shapes with sharp contrast, you place an emphasis on the edges and create a linear feeling. If there is little contrast between the pieces of fabric, and the edges are soft or subtle, the result is less dramatic and may give a suggestion of mystery. With no contrast, you can lose line and shape completely. Missing lines can be used to express subtlety, mystery, or emotion. With this intention, the painted lines in *The Grid Fails* are vague and blend with the background color. In some places they disappear completely and quilting lines take their place.

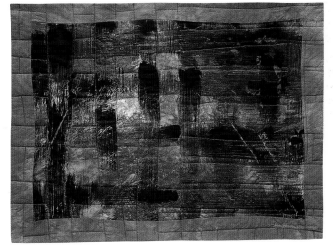

The Grid Fails 32" × 44", 1995. With no contrast, you can lose line and shape completely. The painted lines in this quilt blend with the background color, disappearing completely where quilting lines take their place.

Practice

1. Reduce a design to its basic geometric shapes. Get a full-page magazine advertisement and a fat-tipped black marker. Draw lines with the black pen connecting the points, making large simple shapes: squares, rectangles, triangles, and circles, and tracing the lines. Try another.
2. Look at one of your quilts or a photograph of someone else's quilt. Are the shapes realistic, abstract, or nonobjective? Ask someone else what he or she thinks. Do you agree?
3. Think back on your quilts. Are they mostly straight or curved? Why? Does it have anything to do with your construction methods? Do you want to change that? Do you need to try new construction methods?

Caution, Construction Zone 62" × 60", 1997.

6

❖ ❖ ❖

Value and Color

Value is a word used in design vocabulary to indicate how much light is reflected to the viewer's eye. Pure yellow is a light value and pure blue is a dark value. A yellow may have the same value as a light tan or light gray, and a blue may be the same value as a green or a brown. If a dark color is added to pure yellow, a different yellow is made which is darker in value, that is, it reflects less light. Blue can be made lighter in value by adding clear or white. One important aspect of value is that it is relative. A single color value will appear lighter or darker, depending on what surrounds it.

value
color

Seven Grays The same value gray line is used in the center of each of the blocks. It appears darker in the first block at left than in the block on the far right.

VALUE

The arrangement of values in a composition is important to its success. Obviously, contrast among the values is essential in a black and white composition; otherwise, there would be no design. In a color composition, the hue of the colors distracts the viewer from the values of the colors, but value contrast in a colorful design is also critical. Variation of value in a color design can create a pattern and add complexity that may or may not be noticed by the viewer. The average person can distinguish about forty values, even though there are many more present in the real world. The ability to see the relationship of values in a design with color takes practice, but it is absolutely essential.

Uses of Value
Use Value to Create a Focal Point
Value contrast can be used to create a focal point in the composition. High contrast will attract the viewer's attention. *Stepping Stones in Gray* illustrates the point: your eye is attracted to the upper right corner, the area of the block that has the lightest and darkest colors next to each other.

Stepping Stones in Gray Your eye is attracted to the upper right corner of this quilt block because it is the area of the block that has the greatest contrast: the lightest and darkest colors next to each other.

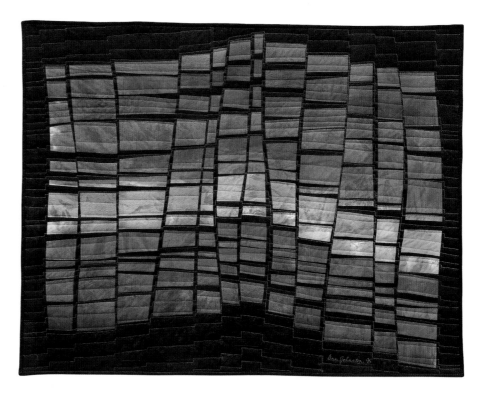

Sunset Strips 3 31″ × 41″, 1995. The viewer's eye immediately goes to the lighter band of color in the center of the quilt where the gold offers the most contrast with the black.

In *Sunset Strips 3*, the viewer's eye immediately goes to the lighter band of color in the center of the quilt because the gold offers the most contrast with black. If that band of lighter color were placed lower in the composition, that's where the attention would center. In fact, the value of a color—that is, the contrast it has with its surrounding values—is often more important to getting attention than what color is chosen. The pieced blocks *Dark Flight* and *Light Flight* show the change in emphasis when only one color is lightened in value. The dark blue area is clearly background to the red line figure in *Dark Flight*. The same blue color in a much lighter value takes over the design of the block in *Light Flight*.

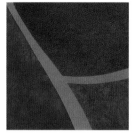

Dark Flight The dark blue area is clearly background to the red line figure in this block.

Light Flight The same blue color in a much lighter value takes over the design in this block.

The placement of value in a block is clear in the example of solid colors. Another consideration is the amount of value contrast in a fabric with a pattern. A fabric with higher value contrast will attract the viewer more than fabric with less value contrast. If you put fabric cut from Orange Sponge in a block, it will command much more attention than if you use a piece from Orange Stones, which has much less value contrast and will thus have a more subtle effect on the viewer.

Orange Sponge Fabric with more value contrast will attract the viewer more than fabric with less value contrast.

Orange Stones This fabric has much less value contrast and would have a more subtle effect if it replaced the brighter colors of Orange Sponge.

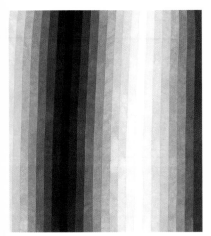

Gray Columns The gradual change from light to dark strips makes it appear that the lightest areas are in front and that they gradually curve back, suggesting depth.

Orange Shape The shape in this block looks flat.

Orange Vase The shading with thread gives dimension to the same shape.

Use Value to Suggest Dimension

Value differences can be used to suggest space, distance, or volume in a composition. The dark blue in the *Dark Flight* block recedes and the light blue in the other sample seems to come forward. The fact that light values usually seem to advance and dark values recede can be used to give dimension to a shape. The gradual change from light to dark strips in *Gray Columns* makes it appear that the lightest areas are in front and that they gradually curve back to the darkest areas.

The impression of dimension and volume can also be created with embroidery. The pieced shape in *Orange Shape* looks flat; after the gradations of light and dark values are added with thread, it looks much rounder. *Orange Vase* has dimension because of the value change.

Use Value for an Emotional Response

Value can be used to evoke an emotional reaction. We associate dark values with sadness, mystery, and seriousness. A quilt with overall dark values and little value contrast will be more likely to fit that description than one with light values and lots of value contrast. *The Grid Fails* (see page 55) is an example of a dark quilt that evokes a mood. The same pieced design can give two completely different impressions: one example, *Dark X*, has only values from medium to dark; the other example *Light X*, has only values from medium to light. There is no doubt that a quilt with overall light values seems more lighthearted, less serious, less threatening.

Using low-value contrast creates a design that seems more subtle, calm, or quiet than a design that uses high contrast. Looking at the *Dark X* and *Light X* blocks illustrates this point. The *Light X* block is more dramatic because the

Dark X This block uses only values from medium to dark, giving it a serious mood.

Light X This block uses only values from medium to light, making it seem more lighthearted, less threatening.

Light X2 In this block, there is no medium value to contrast with the lights, so it is more restrained in mood than *Light X*.

Green Lines 1 This fabric has light, medium, and dark values. This range of contrast makes the fabric more dramatic.

Green Lines 2 This fabric has no extremely light or dark values. Less-value contrast makes it more subtle and understated.

medium value in it contrasts more with the light values than the same medium value contrasts with the dark values in *Dark X*. In *Light X2* there is no medium value to contrast with the lights, so the overall impression given by the block is more restrained. The fabric you choose for a quilt can also be evaluated in the same way. Does it have high-value contrast to give drama or excitement to your quilt, like Green Lines 1? Is the fabric more subtle and calm, with less-value contrast, like Green Lines 2?

COLOR

The color wheel is a circular device designed to help us talk about colors. It is a theory developed to describe the relationship of colors to one another. There have been various other schemes developed, but the familiar twelve-color wheel is fairly simple and it works for most mediums. If you were discussing color precisely, you would need to define what medium you were mixing: light mixes differently than dyes or pigments. For general discussion purposes, the relationships illustrated in this color wheel will work. In Color Triangle, the colors are arranged according to their relationships.

The term *primary colors* refers to the three primary colors, red, yellow, and blue. They are the colors from which other colors are made. They are represented by the three large circles in the Color Triangle. *Secondary colors*, the colors halfway between the primaries, are mixtures of primaries: red and yellow make orange, blue and yellow make green, and red and blue make violet. In the Color Triangle, the secondary colors are represented by three large squares. *Tertiary colors* are mixtures of a primary color and an adjacent secondary color: yellow-green, blue-green, red-violet, blue-violet, red-orange, and yellow-orange. They are represented by the small rectangles in the Color Triangle. *Complementary*

Color Triangle This diagram places the colors according to their relationships. The primary colors are red, yellow, and blue. The secondary colors are orange, green, and violet.

Gray Is Relative The gray appears different in each block because it is surrounded by a different color.

colors are opposites on the color wheel. Each color on the wheel has one that is its opposite. The complements we hear of most often are those of the three primary and secondary colors: yellow and violet, red and green, blue and orange.

Like seeing value, seeing color is relative. How a color appears depends on the colors that surround it. In the pieced blocks *Gray Is Relative*, the same color gray line is placed diagonally across two yellows, two blues, and two reds. The gray appears different in each block because it is surrounded by a different color.

What Color Is Red? The names of the colors mean different things to each of us.

Hue, Value, and Intensity

When you go to your shelf to get some red fabric (What Color Is Red?) what do you mean? What hue, value, and intensity will you be looking for? *Hue* is the name of the color; for example, the hue red comes in many variations, such as hot pink, antique rose, and scarlet. The colors in *Red Swatches* might all be called red, but they are mixtures of the pure hue with other colors. One color can have dozens of names, all subjective, meaning different things to different people. The word *hue* is most often used to refer to the pure color.

All of those reds are not the same value. *Value* refers to the darkness or lightness of a color. A color can be lightened to a pale value, or it can be darkened to a dark value, like the scarlet in the pieced block *Scarlet Values*. The phrases high-key and low-key are sometimes used to describe light and dark values of colors. Each hue has its own "normal value." A pure yellow is a high-key color. That is the nature of yellow. To make yellow darker, it can be mixed with other colors; then it becomes another color, related to yellow, but possibly with a new name. Each color in *Yellow Plus* is a variation of yellow created by the addition of different, very slight, amounts of red and blue.

Intensity refers to the purity of a color. Full intensity means the pure hue of a color. Intensity is also called *saturation*. The yellow in the center of the block *Yellow Plus* is a pure primary yellow. It is 100 percent one color, unmixed. The darker varieties of yellow that surround it are mixed with other colors; they are not 100 percent one color; they do not have the same intensity. That is, they

Red Swatches Each color in this block is the pure hue of red mixed with other colors.

are not as saturated as pure yellow; they are diluted with other colors. Looking at the Color Triangle, the purest colors are the primaries. All the colors in the triangular shape are mixtures of all three primary colors and they are lower in intensity. In *Yellow Plus*, yellow was mixed with different combinations of red and blue; in other words, yellow was mixed with different colors of violet. Yellow was mixed with its complement. Each of the secondary colors is opposite a primary color on the color wheel. When complements are mixed, less intense colors are produced. The color is dulled.

Scarlet Values In this block, scarlet lightens gradually to a pale value, and we give it a different name: pink.

Yellow Plus The color in the center is a pure primary yellow. All the others are variations created by the addition of different, very slight, amounts of red and blue.

The Character of Color

When studying the Color Triangle, it is easy to see that complements are not just opposite in position, but they are opposite in character and temperature as well. Red is hot and green is cool. Blue is calm and orange is quite excited. Yellow is happy, violet is sedate. When complementary hues are placed together, our eyes react: they actually vibrate if you focus closely on the edge for a length of time. A color seems more visually intense when it is placed next to its complement. It is a physical reaction in our eyes that creates this effect, called simultaneous contrast. If the complements are of a different value or intensity, the effect is lessened. In the two Nine-Patches, *Yellow and Purple 1* and *Yellow and Purple 2*, using complementary colors, the difference in value and intensity is significant to the look of each block.

Yellow and Purple 1 When the pure hue of complementary colors are put together, they intensify in our eyes. Simultaneous contrast may make the colors seem to vibrate.

Yellow and Purple 2 If the complements are duller or lighter in value, the effect of simultaneous contrast is not as great.

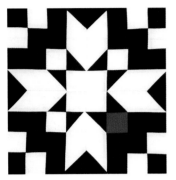

Stepping Stone Your eye goes immediately to the single red piece in the block because color dominates other methods of emphasis, such as size, angle, and placement.

Uses of Color

Use Color for Emphasis

Using color is a direct method to achieve emphasis: color dominates other methods, such as size, angle, and placement. The eye goes immediately to the single red piece in the *Stepping Stone* block. In this example, nothing but its color differentiates the small square that has become the focal of the block. In addition to creating a focal point, color can be used to add accents or to give greater weight to small elements in a design. If the color highlights are small and spread around throughout the composition, they will create a pattern or movement by their placement. *Nathan's Quilt* has patches of red scattered over the whole design. One would have been a focal point, but many are accents that move the eye around the quilt.

Use Color to Indicate Temperature

Use a mix of warm and cool colors to enhance your design. Warm and cool are temperature designations we frequently use for colors that have associations. We identify and relate our senses to colors and give them significance accordingly.

The colors from yellow to orange to red to red-violet on the left side of the Color Triangle are usually thought of as warm or hot colors because of the association of heat with fire and sun. The colors from violet to blue to green to yellow-green on the right side of the Color Triangle are usually considered cool or cold colors because of the association of coolness with sky, water, and plants.

Nathan's Quilt 42" × 36", 1997. If the color highlights are small and spread throughout the composition, they will create a pattern or movement by their placement.

Use Color to Provide Depth

Using cool and warm colors together can give a sense of depth or space to a composition. Because our eyes have a slightly different muscular reaction to different colors as we focus, warm colors seem to advance and cool colors recede. The placement of the colors is important to this effect because the temperature of a color may seem to change when it is placed with different colors. The colors that come forward in a design assume importance and might even seem larger than a shape or line of the same size that is receding.

In the pieced *Horizon Lines*, the white—the lightest color—does come forward, as light colors do, but the red dominates the foreground and the attention because it is the warmest color in the block. This effect is increased because the reds are surrounded by cool grays. The rich red-browns in the lower portion of the block even appear to advance before the cooler blacks next to them. The same principle can be seen in the detail of *Caution: Construction Zone*. All the cool blacks, greens, blues, and yellows make the warm red-orange stand out more than if they all were warmer colors.

Varying color intensity can also be used to give a sense of depth or to flatten a design. The curved shapes in *Come Closer* seem to stretch away into the distance as they get less and less intense. This effect is based on the fact that as objects recede into the distance, they have a more neutral color: that is, they have less intensity of any one color, because dust in the atmosphere breaks up the light rays that are reflected into our eyes. Objects at a distance can seem more bluish, and cooler. This use of intensity and distance works particularly well in a realistic design.

Horizon Lines A sense of space can be enhanced using the contrast of warm and cool. In this block, the white does come forward as light colors do, but the red dominates the foreground and the attention because it is the warmest color in the block.

Caution: Construction Zone, **detail** All the cool blacks, greens, blues, and yellows in this detail make the warm red-orange stand out more than if they all were warmer colors.

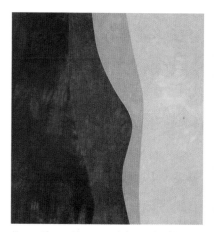

Come Closer The curved shapes in this block seem to stretch away into the distance as they get less and less intense. This effect is based on the fact that, as objects recede into the distance, they acquire a more neutral color.

Warm X All the colors used in this block give it a warm mood.

Cool X Each color in this block has a different degree of coolness.

Use Color to Set a Mood

The temperature of the colors used in a quilt can help set a mood. Color is used as an effective element of design in order to arouse emotions and can be the first aspect that a viewer sees. The warm colors are generally lighter colors and the cool colors darker, so the contrast of emotions is often associated with light and dark. The warm colors can give an immediate sense of warmth, joy, and light. Cool colors give a sense of reserve, sadness, and darkness. This effect is illustrated in *Warm X* and *Cool X*, which use the same composition. The contrast of light and dark is placed in the same pattern, but there is definitely a different feeling expressed in each.

The temperature of the colors used should fit the content of the quilt. The blues and greens in *Leopard Lily* (see page 6) definitely fit the cool mystery of the forest and contrast well with the warm orange colors, making the flowers stand out as the focal point of the quilt. The largest part of *Bird of Paradise* (see page 49) features warm colors and the heavy red accent makes it even warmer. The warm area of color is at the top and is in contrast to the cool colors below to emphasize the feeling of rising. The moods of the two quilts are different and the temperature of the colors used is a major factor in this perception.

Color Relationships

Use the relationships of colors to create an atmosphere in your design. The four basic color relationships are called *color harmonies* or *color schemes*. They are monochromatic, complementary, analogous, and triadic. A monochromatic color scheme uses only one hue with variations in value, and it can tend to create a quiet, cool, and restful feeling as in *Monochromatic Stepping Stones*. A complementary color scheme involves the use of colors opposite each other on the color wheel and creates a lively and exciting design, especially when the colors are the pure hues of primary and secondary colors, as in *Complementary Stepping Stones*. An analogous set of colors uses several hues that are next to each other on the color wheel and gives a related and harmonious feeling, as in *Analogous Stepping Stones*. A

Monochromatic Stepping Stones A monochromatic color scheme uses only one hue with variations in value, and it can tend to create a quiet, cool, and restful feeling.

Complementary Stepping Stones A complementary color scheme uses colors opposite each other on the color wheel and creates a lively and exciting design, especially when pure hues of primary and secondary colors are used.

Analogous Stepping Stones An analogous set of colors uses several hues that are next to each other on the color wheel and conveys a related and harmonious feeling.

Triadic Stepping Stones A triadic color scheme uses three hues equally spaced on the color wheel and usually creates a contrasting and lively design.

triadic color scheme uses three hues equally spaced on the color wheel, and usually creates a contrasting and lively design, as in *Triadic Stepping Stones*. If a quilt design is particularly complex, using one of these color harmonies might work to unify the design. Conversely, a simple quilt can handle a complex color scheme.

The use of an unexpected color rather than the "real" color of an object can add interest or help communicate the idea behind a design. In *Trillium Too*, I used the actual color, sometimes called local color, of the flower and the leaves as they were in the forest behind my house, shown in Forest Flower.

Trillium Too 33″ × 47″, 1990. Hand quilted by Diane Roberts. I used the actual color of the flower and the leaves as I saw them growing.

Forest Flower A detail of the trillium in the forest. Photograph by the author.

Trillium 3 29" × 32", 1992. Hand quilted by Diane Roberts. I used unexpected colors when I wanted to make the flower petals pop out.

In *Trillium 3*, I used unexpected colors for the same flower. I wanted to make the flower petals pop out and make all the leaves different colors. Sometime, I will try this design in other color combinations to get other effects.

Even the placement of colors that have no basic affinity for each other—*color discord*—can add visual interest, excitement, or make a point about the content of the quilt. The colors with the least affinity for each other are those that are widely separated on the color wheel but are not complements, like the blue-green and yellow-orange in *Caution: Construction Zone* (see page 56). This is how I feel every time I walk through an area under construction. Color discord is greater when the value is the same; few color combinations are discordant if they vary greatly in value and intensity.

Colors may be chosen with no regard for their subject matter. They can be chosen solely to enhance the design and for esthetic or emotional reasons. When I built *North Is Up* (see page 1), I started with the gold fabric because I like gold and I wanted it to stand out. The rest of the color decisions I made for the quilt were based on what colors provided the right amount of contrast and created the atmosphere I wanted.

VALUE AND COLOR ARE RELATIVE

The differences between hues in a design are fairly easy to see. Value differences are not always so easy to determine. When you pick a color of fabric, you also pick a value. Since value is the more subtle of the two, I think it is important to

North Is Up, **detail** I quilted heavily over the bright green grid lines with dark thread to darken them and lessen their visual impact.

pay as much attention to value as to color. The hue of a color will get our immediate attention, but the subtle value pattern within a color design will determine how interesting the whole design is to the viewer. *Scott's Square* (see page 45) uses bright, intense colors; the actual values of those colors can be seen in this black and white photo of the whole quilt. Looking at the whole quilt without colors, the value pattern shows up much more clearly. The quilt has several large and many small shapes of light value: they stand out sharply against the other shapes, which are mostly dark and medium values.

Once the fabric is chosen and assembled, quilters have still more choices of surface treatments, including quilting, couching, painting, and beading, that will influence the colors as well as the values in a quilt. After I finished piecing, quilting, and binding *North Is Up*, I decided that the yellow-green was too bright and stood out too much. So instead of quilting around it like I might have, I quilted over it with dark thread, as you can see in the detail shown here, to darken the color value.

Scott's Quilt Looking at the whole quilt without colors, the value pattern shows up much more clearly. The quilt has several large and many small shapes of very light value that stand out sharply against the other shapes—mostly dark and medium values.

Practice

1. Take some colored, patterned fabrics to the copy store and make black/gray/white copies. Make sure the copies are photo grade. Stack the copies in order of darkest to lightest overall value. Then, rearrange them in order of least to most value contrast. Which task was harder?

2. Using photographs of your quilts, make black/gray/white copies. Rate each one on a scale of one to three: little value contrast is a one, some value contrast a two, and lots of value contrast a three. How do you work—using lots of value contrast or very little? Would you like to change that?

3. Look at five of your favorite quilts—yours or those of other people. What color predominates in each? Are they generally the same color or different? What colors do you most like to use or see in quilts? Do you want to achieve a mood effect? Temperature effect? Eye-popping effect?

Balancing Act 9 30" × 40", 1998.

P

7

Pattern and Texture

The words *pattern* and *texture* are often used interchangeably because a pattern may give a surface the appearance of texture and because textures have a distinct repeating arrangement that creates a pattern. *Pattern* is a repetitive design with the same motif appearing in a predictable way. The repetition of the motif, color, value, line, shape, or texture, however, does not necessarily have to be identical in order to create a pattern. This quilt block from *Balancing Act 9* has fabrics with several patterns. Each has considerable variety in color and value but remains predictable and distinct.

attern

Texture

First Block This quilt block from *Balancing Act 9*, in progress, has fabrics with several patterns. Each pattern has considerable variety in color and value within it but remains predictable and distinct.

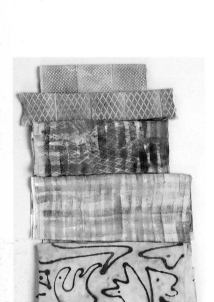

Gold/Green Silks The scale of the pattern moves from small scale in the top piece to large scale in the bottom piece.

PATTERN

A quilter can use design elements such as solid colors and plain thread without any pattern in them, and use them in a way that creates a pattern in the whole composition. If you look at *Stepping Stones Repeated* (see page 16), it is easy to see a pattern made by the small squares and triangles. The color value, scale, and placement of the elements you use will affect the pattern outcome.

Fabric with a pattern may be used to contribute to the unity, balance, or variety in the design, but the *scale* of the pattern, that is, its size in relationship to the size of the pieces that are cut, will determine the impact of the pattern on the overall design of the quilt. If the fabric has a large scale pattern, its repetitions will not even be visible when small pieces are cut from it. If the fabric has a medium scale pattern, the repeats may be visible and be a strong part of the design. Differences of scale are simple to see in the fabric pictured in Gold/Green Silks. The scale of the pattern moves from small in the top piece to large in the bottom piece. The large scale pattern will not show at all if the pieces are cut too small.

It is important to remember that the size of the fabric pattern will influence its readability at a distance. If the scale of the pattern is tiny, the impact of the pattern on the viewer may not be its distinct individuality, but rather a subtle contrast of value or color in the area it is used. The small patterning in the reds is only visible at close range in the detail of *New Persian*. Compare the detail to the overall photo of the quilt on page 4. At a distance, the pattern becomes part of the character of the color and value of the fabric and has no influence as pattern.

New Persian, detail The small-scale pattern in the reds is only visible at close range.

Types of Pattern

Patterns can be broadly grouped into categories according to their style or shape. Is the pattern geometric or amorphous: that is, does it have mostly straight lines with angles, or does the pattern have mostly curves, or curved shapes? The pattern in *Square Rainbows* is made up of straight lines, squares, and rectangles. Even though some parts of the pattern do not have ruler-straight lines, it is a geometric pattern. The repeating white curves in *Waterfalls* definitely put this fabric pattern in the curvilinear category.

A pattern can be realistic, abstract, or nonobjective. It might look exactly like flowers or animals, or it might be an abstraction, suggesting the subject with simple lines and shapes, as in Stones and Women. The pattern in The Oculate Being is a more extreme example of an abstract design. The eye and mouth are clearly represented, but the arms and legs and body have taken on abstract geometric shapes. Both Black and White Plaid and Short Ladders are examples of nonobjective patterns.

Square Rainbows The pattern is made up of straight lines, squares, and rectangles. Even though some of the parts of the pattern do not have ruler-straight lines, it is a geometric pattern.

Waterfalls The pattern on this fabric is curvilinear.

Stones and Women The pattern on this fabric is an abstraction, simplified shapes that suggest the subjects.

The Oculate Being The pattern is an extreme abstraction of a human body. The eyes and mouth can be seen in the semicircles and the body, arms, and legs in the triangles and volutes.

Black and White Plaid This fabric has a rigid, nonobjective pattern.

Short Ladders The lines and shapes of color create a flowing, nonobjective pattern.

Patterns may also be referred to as rigid or flowing, geometric or curvilinear. Although both The Oculate Being and Black and White Plaid samples have geometric shapes and lines, they are distinct and precise compared to the flowing shapes and lines in Stones and Women and Short Ladders. The character of the patterns you choose, whether realistic, abstract, or nonobjective, whether flowing or rigid, will influence the overall look of your quilt.

Uses of Pattern

Use a pattern to create a shape or a line. In this sample piece of fabric, Random Rectangles, the pattern of short lines changes direction, creating the shape of a rectangle which repeats all over the fabric. The rectangle seems to take predominance. The brief discontinuance of the pattern in Interrupted creates a horizontal line above the middle of the printed design.

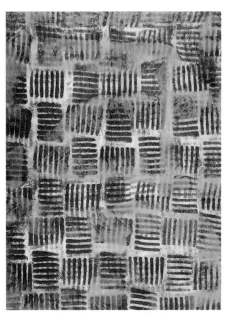

Random Rectangles The pattern of short lines changes direction, creating rectangular shapes that repeat all over the fabric.

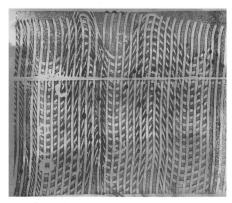

Interrupted Just the discontinuance of the pattern creates a horizontal line through the printed design.

Use Pattern to Set a Mood

Use patterns in your quilts to set a mood. If the patterns are rigid or geometric, the design will have a different impact on the viewer than if the patterns are amorphous and flowing. The mood of one pattern can be used to contrast with the mood of another in order to emphasize a point you want to make in the design. In Black and White Curtain, the small diamond pattern, repeated, in turn creates a checkerboard pattern, contrasting sharply with the curvilinear pattern that emerges occasionally from behind the checkerboard. The viewer is attracted to the side with the most dominant patterns, rather than to the side with the irregular dark and light areas.

Use pattern to add interest in areas of a design. If you look closely at the detail of Black and White Curtain, the places where the eye seems most attracted are the places where the dotted pattern becomes apparent. In this case, the small areas of pattern are scattered accents. The placement of a pattern or the absence of a pattern can create a focal point or an accent to a design. In *Green and Gold*, the pieces in the block with the large pattern of bold black lines stand out more than the pieces with the smaller pattern. All the patterned areas attract more interest than the solid pieces.

Green and Gold The placement of a pattern or the absence of a pattern can create a focal point or an accent to a design.

Black and White Curtain The repetition of the small diamond creates a checkerboard pattern, contrasting sharply with the curvilinear pattern that emerges occasionally from behind the checkerboard. The viewer is attracted to the side with the most dominant patterns.

Use Pattern for Unity

A quilter can use pattern (or another design element) to divide one part of a composition from another or to tie parts together. The dark blue and purple areas of the fabric in the coat *Red and Blue Velveteen* are divided irregularly by areas of light values, but the design is tied together by the repetition of the grid pattern and the wood block prints that continue across the dark and light areas. In the small quilt *In Anticipation* (see page 86), the fabric with a dark green-and-yellow grid pattern occurs in several small pieces and on both sides of the center portion of the main design. This repetition of pattern makes the disjointed pieces seem to be part of a whole background for the blue strips scattered over it.

Use Pattern to Show Depth

Pattern can be used to give a sense of depth by changing the pattern scale in the design. Large scale patterns often seem to be in the foreground and small scale patterns in the background, as in *Green and Gold*. Overlapping patterns also provide a sense of depth, as if the viewer is seeing through one pattern to another. In *Red and Blue Velveteen*, the diagonal grid pattern and the random swirl pattern occur in the same place, making it appear that one is behind the other and adding a sense of depth. When the patterns have a different scale, the effect is emphasized. An example of this is seen in detail 2 of Black and White Curtain, where the tiny diamond grid overlaps the circles and wood block prints.

Red and Blue Velveteen Hand-dyed and machine-quilted cotton velveteen coat, 1998.

Red and Blue Velveteen The diagonal grid and the random swirl occur in the same places, making it appear that one is behind the other and adding a sense of depth.

Black and White Curtain, detail When the patterns have a different scale, the effect of depth is emphasized.

Use Quilting to Create Pattern

Pattern and texture are inseparable when it comes to quilting. The pattern chosen for the quilting stitches creates a certain kind of texture. If it is a curvilinear pattern, the wrinkles in the fabric will appear different than if the stitch pattern is rectilinear. Whether you choose a pattern that varies in density of quilting or one that is an evenly spaced, open pattern will also affect the texture of the quilt.

Both *Leaves 2* and *Nathan's Quilt* are machine quilted with various colors of thread. In the details of the quilt backs, it is apparent that the texture created by the quilting patterns has much more visual effect than the thread colors. In *Leaves 2* the pattern is curvilinear and varied in density. Where the small shapes fill the spaces, the larger unquilted areas are wrinkled by the quilted shapes around them. In *Nathan's Quilt* the stitching is rectilinear and evenly spaced, giving an even texture without emphasizing any part of the quilt.

Leaves 2, back The quilting pattern is curvilinear and varied in density. While the small shapes fill the spaces, the larger unquilted areas are textured by the quilted shapes around them.

Nathan's Quilt, back The stitching is rectilinear and evenly spaced, giving an even texture without emphasizing any part of the quilt.

TEXTURE

Texture is the nature of a material's surface. Is it smooth and shiny like satin, ridged like corduroy, rough like burlap, or fuzzy like flannel? We usually appreciate texture through our sense of touch; however, we also recognize texture visually. For the purposes of discussion here, I will use the term *tactile texture* to refer to that which can actually be felt; that is, the weave of the fabric or the embroidery or beading on a quilt. I will use the term *visual texture* for that which can be seen and gives the appearance of a texture where no actual difference in the surface can be felt. Examples of visual texture are printed fabrics that look like rock or sand, but actually feel smooth and even.

The photograph of the fabric Cracked and Scratched gives the appearance of a highly textured surface, scored and covered with crackle. The fabric is actually a smooth cotton broadcloth, dyed to give that appearance. Using this fabric would add visual texture to an area of a design. The *Balancing Act 9* block shown on page 72 has texture created with quilting stitches. The solid colors in the quilt have some visual texture and are highlighted by the tactile texture created by the quilting stitches.

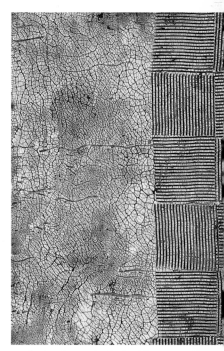

Cracked and Scratched This fabric gives the appearance of a highly textured surface, scored and covered with crackle. It adds visual texture to a quilt.

Blue and Green Threads Just looking at some of the threads available will give you ideas. The different weights and textures of the threads will add texture and dimension to a design.

Architects may be interested in varying the texture of walls on a building. They may use the contrast in textures of smooth river rocks and rough peeled-log poles. A painter may emphasize texture by applying thick paint. A weaver may use thick, thin, coarse, or smooth yarn to provide contrast of texture. Quilters have the advantage of being able to choose from a whole range of fabrics, embellishments, and quilting and construction techniques to achieve a variety of textures. A hundred years ago quilters were taking advantage of fancy fabrics, embroidery stitches, paint, lace, and ribbons. We have even more options today, especially in threads, and we can use them to enhance our quilt designs. Just looking at some of the threads available will give you ideas. The different weights and textures shown in Blue and Green Threads are waiting for the right quilt.

Like pattern, visual distance is a factor in how much texture is seen by a viewer. The quilt *North Is Up* (see page 1) is partly appliquéd and is quilted in various patterns all over, very heavily in some places. Viewed from just a few feet away, the zigzag pattern of quilting over the yellow-green grid lines and over the edges of the appliquéd compass arrow blend into the overall image; however, you can see more texture in the detail on page 33. It is important to remember when planning a large quilt that its textural qualities will add visual interest to the design at close range and will have much less impact at a distance.

Roots This organic design was created using couching, reverse appliqué, and wrinkled fabric.

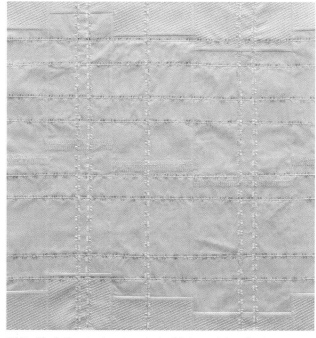

White Block Structural textures in the fabrics and threads were used to create the design in this block.

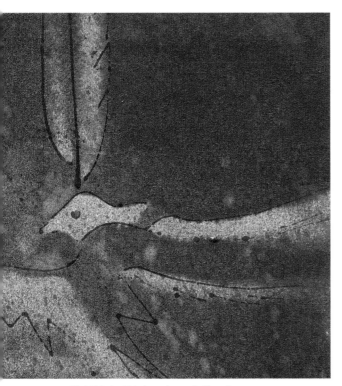

Bird Fabric This is a piece of silk noil with some nubby texture to it, but no embellishment.

Birds 9 16″ × 13″, 1995. This piece uses raw-edge appliqué and several different machine-quilting patterns to add texture. The rectilinear appliqué contrasts sharply with the curves of the painted fabric and sets off the lower left corner.

Types of Texture

Textures can be generally organized into two types: amorphous—organic and curvilinear—or structural—rigid and geometric. We can choose from a huge array of fabric types to add texture to our quilts: from cheesecloth to velvet to felt. In the white block *Roots* the entire design is created with variations in fabrics, stitches, and embellishments. The lines are curving and organic. In *White Block*, the lines are all regular and rectilinear, very structural. The effect given by the two different types of texture is completely distinct. The contrast you may wish to use might be more subtle or even bolder.

Uses of Texture

Use texture to add impact to the design of the quilt. Like the other elements, line, shape, color, value, and pattern, texture can help define the design and contribute to its success. Bird Fabric is a piece of silk noil that has some nubby texture to it, but no embellishment. A small finished quilt, *Birds 9*, is made from another piece of the same fabric; it features raw-edge appliqué and several different machine-quilting patterns to add texture. The appliqué contrasts sharply with the curves of the painted fabric and sets off the lower left corner, at the same time suggesting landscape seen from the air.

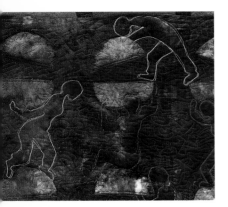

Balancing Act 7, **detail** The shapes of the people are created by a double outline of heavier thread.

Use Texture to Suggest Movement

Texture can be used to create lines and a sense of movement. In *Birds 9*, the spiral quilting lines add swirls and shapes in the sky and the long, wavy, diagonal quilting lines interrupting the pattern in the middle suggest motion and contribute to the idea of a bird in flight. The lines of quilting not only add a line of thread color, they create lines and shapes of texture, raised areas, and wrinkles in a quilt's surface. The shapes of the people in the detail of *Balancing Act 7* did not exist in the design of the quilt top when it was finished. They are created by a double line outlining a shape. The lines stand out more than the background quilting because they contrast in color and are quilted with heavy (size 30) thread.

Use Texture to Add Dimension

Texture can be used to enhance shapes and to add dimension in a quilt design. In *Balancing Act 8*, detail in progress, some texture has been added to make the rocks look rounder and to emphasize their cracks. In the detail from the finished quilt, *Balancing Act 8*, more machine embroidery adds to the dimension of the rocks; quilting lines of metallic thread add lines and shapes to the background that suggest water in motion.

The texture of surface stitching can not only give dimension to a shape, but it can also give the impression of depth by overlapping a pattern underneath. The detail from *Red and Blue Velveteen* shows how the layer of quilting stitches adds a new layer of pattern and a sense of transparency to that which was present on the unquilted fabric (see page 76). The quilting is done on velveteen, adding to the impression made by the thread in the surface and giving a greater sense of texture.

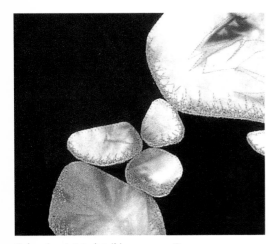

Balancing Act 8, **detail in progress** Some texture has been added to make the rocks look rounder and to emphasize their cracks.

Balancing Act 8, **detail** Machine embroidery adds dimension to the rocks and quilting lines of metallic thread add lines and shapes to the background, suggesting water in motion.

Red and Blue Velveteen, **detail** A layer of quilting stitches adds another pattern *over* the pattern on the unquilted fabric. Because the quilting is done on velveteen, the thread makes a deeper impression in the surface, giving a greater sense of texture.

Techniques Influence Texture

The construction techniques that a quilter chooses have a great influence on the texture of a quilt. Piecing in and of itself creates visible edges with shadows on a quilt top. A whole-cloth quilt will have a much flatter look than one with seams or appliqué.

There are many kinds of appliqué and each has a different quality and degree of texture. Hand appliqué with turned-under edges looks more dimensional than fused appliqué with flat edges. Between those two types of appliqué there are many variations, each with its own texture: turned-under edges with invisible thread hemstitching; raw-edge appliqué with hand-embroidered buttonhole stitches; raw-edge appliqué with threads hanging out; and fused appliqué with heavy machine satin stitch around the edges. The wrinkles and texture created by traditional hand appliqué in *My Impossible Garden*, detail 1, have a completely different appearance than the flat look of the fused raw-edge appliqué in the detail of *Sunset Strips 5*.

Embellishments of all kinds add texture. Embroidery by hand or machine, beads, paint, and heavy threads are a few examples. The possibilities are limitless. Hand embroidery gives dimension to the tiny wildflowers in *My Impossible Garden*, second detail. A combination of fused appliqué, machine embroidery, machine quilting, and glitter give texture to *Night Falls* (see page 114).

My Impossible Garden, detail 1 105" × 94", 1988. The wrinkling and texture created by traditional hand appliqué has a distinctive look, completely different from the flat look of fused appliqué.

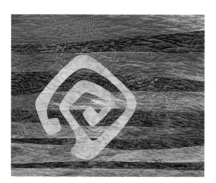

Sunset Strips 5, detail Fused appliqué with zigzag quilting makes a flatter design than hand appliqué with edges turned under.

My Impossible Garden, detail 2 Hand embroidery gives dimension, as well as texture, to the small flowers in the design.

Crimson Tide, detail 26" × 34", 1988. The
embossed background texture is created
entirely with various patterns of hand quilting, using light colors of silk thread.

Begonia, detail 21" × 17", 1988. Different
effects can be created by the choice of
thread and stitch length for hand quilting.
The tiny stitches form lines to enhance the
shapes of the flower petals, while shiny silk
thread attracts the eye to the long stitches.

Balancing Act II, detail The small puckers
around the feet are a hand-stitched line, and
the large "X" shapes and long, irregular gold
stitches are also hand quilted. Machine quilting in the ditch around the piecing gives a
firm-looking line. See the full quilt on page 10.

The type of quilting used changes the texture of a quilt: a hand-quilted line
looks a lot different than a machine-quilted line. The detail of *Begonia* shows the
different effects that can be created by choice of thread and stitch length for hand
quilting. The tiny stitches form lines to enhance the shapes of the flower petals,
and the shiny silk thread attracts the eye to the long stitches. The embossed texture in the background of *Crimson Tide* is created entirely with various patterns
of hand quilting using light colors of silk thread to make the stitches slightly more
visible than if they were white.

Machine quilting makes a much
firmer, hard line than hand stitches.
There are examples of both in the detail
of *Balancing Act II*. The small puckers
around the feet are a hand-stitched line
and the large "X" shapes and long, irregular gold stitches are also hand quilted.
There is machine stitch-in-the-ditch
around the piecing, providing a hard,
firm-looking line. The type of quilting
should be determined by how you want
the quilt to look. In the detail of #146,
Rock Garden IV, the density of the
machine stitches in the dark lines makes

a flat area, contrasting with the unquilted shapes of the rocks and causing them to stand out more from the surface of the quilt; in turn, this effect, adds a real shadow in the dark cracks between the rocks.

PATTERN AND TEXTURE IN QUILTS

Texture and pattern have a great number of uses: they can create lines, create shapes, set a mood, unify, and add variety. Use contrast of texture and pattern to create visual interest and focal points, especially in large quilts. Quilters should consider both pattern and texture in the choices of fabrics and threads, construction and quilting techniques, and embellishments. I think that the importance of these choices is largely underestimated by quilters.

Any design you might want to create can be achieved in more than one way. For example, when I plan a quilt now, I usually think of piecing first. I pieced in all the grid lines in *North Is Up* (see page 1). Why didn't I use appliqué? It would have added a layer of new texture, especially if I left the raw edges. Fused appliqué would have been quicker, too, I think. I will find out in one of my next quilts. When I decided that *Sunset Strips 5*, in progress, needed more gold and more texture, I had many choices: shiny paint, glitter, beads, gold foil, and various gold threads.

#146, Rock Garden IV, **detail** The density of the machine stitches in the dark lines creates a flat area that contrasts with the unquilted shapes of the rocks, thus causing them to stand out more from the surface of the quilt. This adds a real shadow in the dark cracks between the rocks.

Practice

1. How many places do you see contrast of pattern in your latest quilt? What kinds of patterns are they? Look at the quilt from a distance of ten feet and answer again.

2. Choose one of your quilts that has the most texture. How would you categorize the textures you used? Mostly amorphous or mostly structural? Or both? Could the quilt be improved with more of one than the other?

3. List the construction, quilting, and embellishment techniques you usually use when making a quilt; for example, piecing, hand appliqué, glitter glue, couching, and so forth. List the techniques you want to try sometime. Use one of them in your next quilt.

PART 3

Making
Design
Decisions

Coriolis Effect 84" × 66", 1998.

In Anticipation 23" × 23", 1997.

P

8

❖ ❖ ❖

Practice, Practice, Practice

Just as you build a large vocabulary through lots of reading, you also build a large collection of images through lots of observation. You learn how letters and words work together (spelling and grammar) to create paragraphs and whole books by reading them. You also learn how lines and shapes, colors and values, patterns and textures create compositions by looking at artworks. Every opportunity you have to observe is an opportunity to learn.

ractice

OBSERVE, QUESTION, AND LEARN

When you observe, you should ask yourself questions that are directed toward what you want to learn. If you want to learn about balance, ask yourself some questions about balance while you are looking at a particular painting or quilt. When you are making a quilt, ask yourself questions before you start, while you are making the quilt, and after it is done. I look at each quilt as a step in the process of learning, not as an end in itself. As I make each quilt, I observe what happens and when finished, I learn more. The next quilt will be a product of that learning.

I started and finished *In Anticipation* while I was making *North Is Up* (see page 1). I wanted to practice, just to see what would happen, with different piecing techniques and quilting designs. This helped me decide what to do in *North Is Up*.

The main questions are: How can I make this quilt look like my idea? How do I make it look like I want it to? What things can I do to make the idea come across to the viewer? My answer is to use the designer's elements of line, shape, value, color, pattern, and texture effectively. Which element should I use, and when should I use it? There is no limit to the variables. My attitude is to use as many as I can to see what happens, to learn by doing. It has been said that if we see something, we are ten times more likely to remember it than if we hear it. Practice takes time and work, but it is exciting and fun.

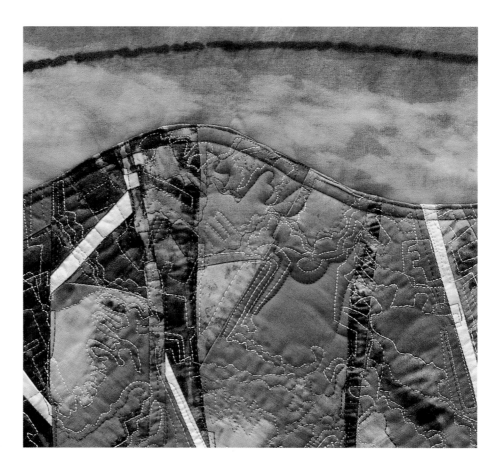

In Anticipation, detail.

PRACTICE ONE

This is an opportunity to practice what you know about design. Each photograph will have several questions that are based on the information in the first six chapters in this book. Read the questions and answer the ones that seem obvious to you. Then try the questions that seem more difficult. If you cannot think of an answer, just skip the question and come back to it later. These are not trick questions, they are open-ended questions: there is more than one good answer to each of them. You may decide to note your answers and see if you agree with yourself at a later date.

Untitled 1

- What is the main design element: line, shape, value, color, pattern, or texture?
- What element would you change about this design to make it more interesting to you?
- What kind of *balance* does this design have? Formal, informal, radial, or allover?
- What kinds of pattern are used in this design? Are they organic/flowing or structural/rigid?

Untitled 2

- What kind of *lines* are used in this design? Actual lines, implied lines, or mental lines? Describe the lines.
- What kind of *values* are used in this design? Light, dark, high-contrast, low-contrast? Describe them.
- Where is the *visual weight* in this design?
- Compare the kinds of *rhythm* used in *Untitled 1* and *Untitled 2*. Static, alternating, or progressive? Smooth or uneven?

Untitled 1 What kind of *balance* does this design have?

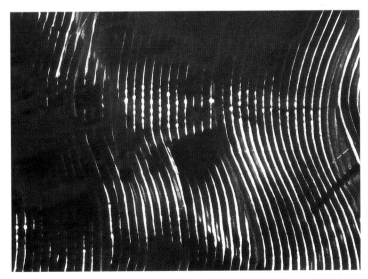

Untitled 2 What kind of *lines* are used in this design?

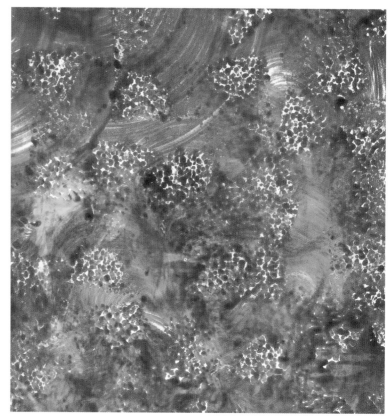

Untitled 3 What kind of *colors* are used in this design?

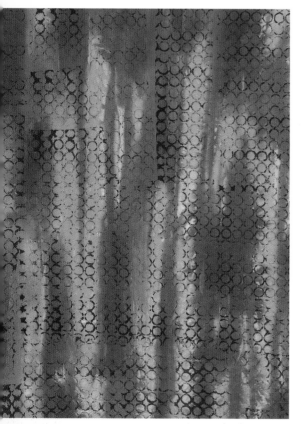

Untitled 4 What kind of *shapes* are used in this design?

Untitled 3

- What is the *main* design element? Line, shape, value, color, pattern, or texture?
- What kind of *colors* are used in this design? Warm/cool, bright/dull? Describe them.
- What kinds of *contrast* do you see in this design? Value, color, size, texture, pattern, line direction, style?
- What would you change about this design to make it more interesting to you?

Untitled 4

- What kind of *colors* are used in this design? Warm/cool, intense/dull? Describe them.
- What type of *color scheme* is used in this design? Monochromatic, analogous, complementary, or triadic?
- What kind of *shapes* are used in this design? Describe them.
- Compare the similarities and differences between *Untitled 3* and *Untitled 4*. Thinking of all the designer's elements, which is the one most important to making them different?

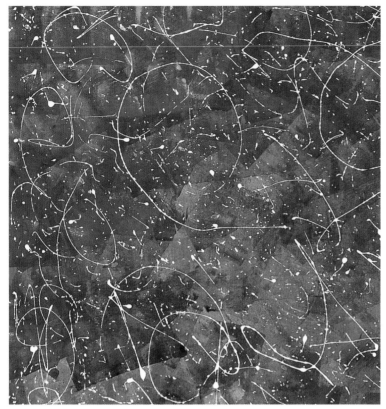

Untitled 5 Which kind of *contrast* is most important to the overall impact of this design?

Untitled 6 Where is the *visual weight* in this design?

Untitled 5

- What kind of *lines* are used in this design? Actual lines, implied lines, or mental lines? Describe the lines.
- How do the *lines* contribute to the design?
- What kind of *colors* are used in this design? Warm/cool, bright/dull? Describe them.
- What kind of *values* are used in this design? High-key, low-key, high-contrast, low-contrast? Describe them.
- Which kind of *contrast* is most important to the overall impact of this design?
- What design element is used to accomplish a sense of mood or motion?

Untitled 6

- Where is the *visual weight* in this design?
- Do you like this design? What *elements* (line, shape, value, color, pattern, or texture) in the design attract or repel you?
- Which kind of *contrast* is most important to the overall impact of this design?
- What design element is used to accomplish a sense of depth and rhythm?
- Compare the use of *lines* in *Untitled 5* and *Untitled 6*, noting the type of lines and their function.

Untitled 7 What is the function of *value contrast* in the design?

Untitled 8 Does this design have a *focal point*?

Untitled 7

- What kind of *shapes* are used in this design? Real, distorted, abstract, or nonrepresentational? Describe the shapes.
- What kind of *colors* are used in this design? Warm/cool, bright/dull? Describe them.
- What is the function of *value contrast* in the design?
- What part of the design seems to be the foreground? What part the background?

Untitled 8

- Does this design have a *focal point*? What part is it?
- Is this design balanced or unbalanced? What makes it so?
- Which elements in this design seem to be grouped, creating unity through proximity?
- What kinds of *contrast* do you see in this design? Value, color, size, texture, pattern, line direction, style?
- Is there a distracting element in this design?
- Compare the complexity of the patterns in *Untitled 7* and *Untitled 8*. How does it affect the viewer? Which is more successful?

Untitled 9 What does *value contrast* contribute to the design?

Untitled 9

- What kind of *balance* does this design have? Formal, informal, radial, or allover?
- What kind of *patterns* are used in this design, amorphous or structural? Are they flowing or rigid?
- What does *value contrast* contribute to the design?
- Does this design have *unity*? What ties it all together?
- How is a sense of depth achieved in this design? Placement in design, size, overlapping, value of color, intensity of color?

Untitled 10

- Is this design *balanced* or *unbalanced*? What makes it so?
- Which kind of *contrast* is most important to the overall impact of this design? Value, color, size, texture, pattern, line direction?
- What design element is used to accomplish a sense of emotion or emphasis?
- Compare *Untitled 9* and *Untitled 10*. What important design *elements* do they share? Which design element differentiates them?

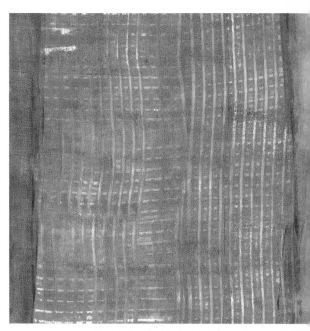

Untitled 10 Is this design *balanced* or *unbalanced*?

Untitled 11 What kind of *rhythm* does this design have?

Untitled 12 Which kind of *contrast* is most important to the overall impact of this design?

Untitled 11

- What is the main design element? Line, shape, value, color, pattern, or texture?
- What kind of *rhythm* does this design have? Static, alternating, or progressive? Is it smooth or uneven?
- What kind of *shapes* are used in this design? Real, distorted, abstract, or nonrepresentational? Describe the shapes.
- Which elements in this design seem to be grouped, creating unity through proximity?

Untitled 12

- What kind of *patterns* are used in this design? Amorphous or structural, flowing or rigid? Describe the shapes.
- How are the *accents* created in this design? What design element creates them?
- Does this design have *unity*? What ties it all together?
- Which kind of *contrast* is most important to the overall impact of this design?
- Compare how a sense of *depth* is achieved in *Untitled 11* and *Untitled 12*. Placement in design, size, overlapping, value of color, intensity of color?

PRACTICE TWO

Pull out some of the quilts you have made and answer these questions about each.

1. What impact did I want to make with this quilt?
2. What is the *main* design element of the quilt? Line, shape, value, color, pattern, or texture?
3. How did other elements of the design contribute to the overall effect?
4. What part of the quilt commands most attention? Does this focal point enhance the quilt design?
5. Does any line, shape, or texture distract from the intended effect? How could that distraction become a contribution to the design?
6. What do I like best about this quilt design? What element of design is it? Do I use this element a lot in my other quilts?
7. Does this quilt have balance? What kind? Does it fit the quilt or should I have used a different kind of balance?
8. Does this quilt have unity? What ties the elements of the design together or separates them too much?
9. Does this quilt have variety? Enough or too much? Which kind?
10. If I did this quilt again, how would I make it different? Why?

I'll go first and answer some questions about *In Anticipation* (see page 86).

What is the *main* design element of the quilt?

I think shape is the main design element of *In Anticipation*. There are some important lines in the quilt, but the centerpiece is a large amorphous shape that extends beyond the edges.

What part of the quilt commands most attention? Does this focal point enhance the quilt design?

I think the long curved top edge of the central shape is the focal point of the quilt because it contrasts so sharply with the soft blurry shape and light values behind it. I do think it is an anticipatory kind of line, rising at the right edge.

Does this quilt have unity? What ties the elements of the design together or separates them too much?

The quilt is unified mostly by color and color values, but the repetition of line and pattern also works to unify it.

If I did this quilt again, how would I make it different? Why?

When I stitched the foreground piece to the background piece, I used a machine stitch which gives it a hard edge and attaches it tightly to the background. If I had sewn it by hand with a blind stitch, the shape would seem to float more in front, giving an increased sense of depth.

PRACTICE THREE

Here are a few small projects to promote experience through practice. They provide an opportunity to do something and see what happens. They are not designed to start a quilt. Please enjoy them and make any adaptations to the projects that you wish.

Line Project

Gather 10 to 15 sheets of unlined white paper. Think of an emotion or feeling and draw black lines (not shapes) that express that emotion. Use as many sheets as it takes to make one that you think someone else could interpret correctly. Try it out on someone to see if he or she agrees.

Try the same exercise, but use only one line on each sheet of paper. Pay attention to the type of pen or marker you use: its width, it values, and the shapes of the lines it makes. Two examples of whimsical lines are shown in Thin Line and Thick Line.

Options

1. Trace one of your lines onto white fabric and stitch it with decorative embroidery stitches (machine or hand), or couch a heavy textured yarn along the same path as the line.

2. Put fusible web on the back of some black fabric and try the same exercise by cutting out a line with scissors. Move it around on a piece of white fabric to decide the best position for it before you iron it down.

Shape Project

Cut out an 18″ square of a dark fabric (solid or print, black if you wish). We will call this dark piece background. Cut out 6 to 20 shapes of light fabric (solid or print, white if you wish). They may be all similar shapes or very different from each other. We will call these shapes foreground. Place the light shapes on the dark background block and move them around. Ask these questions: When do the shapes make a figure in the foreground? When does the arrangement create a figure out of the background? Which is harder? When does the arrangement of the shapes create no figure in foreground or background? When does the arrangement of shapes create a design in both the foreground and the background? *Chimu Window* and *Chimu Wall* are two samples from a set of shapes I used to answer some of these questions. Also refer to *Crossroads* and *Four Kites* on page 15 for another example of a background/foreground reversal.

Thin Line Whimsical line, dyed with a needle-nosed bottle.

Thick Line Whimsical line, looking more serious dyed with a wide sponge brush.

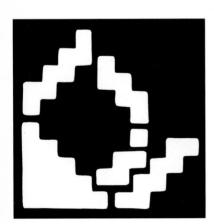

Chimu Window When does the arrangement create a figure out of the background?

Chimu Wall When does the arrangement of shapes create a design in both the foreground and the background?

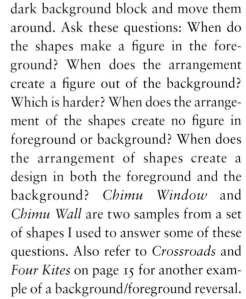

Options

1. Take photographs of your arrangements. Choose one arrangement: either piece or fuse the shapes into one of the choices you liked.

2. Put together three more of the same block and see how they fit together. Take photographs of the arrangements you like, choose one, and sew it together.

Value Project

Make a black and white photocopy of a block that you have made—if you have something left over from another quilt, all the better. Look for a pattern of values and decide how it might be improved. Now change the values of different parts of the block by any method you can devise. Make dark areas lighter or light areas darker. Among the possibilities are overlays of transparent or opaque fabrics, light or heavy embroidery or quilting, painting, beads, foils, or couching threads. Change the design completely by changing the values in different parts of the block. Compare the value patterns in both pieces and, if you wish, change the values further. Try to make the variations in light and dark areas more interesting than the original block. Make another photocopy of the block.

Scott's Square, **black and white** A black and white print of *Scott's Square* shows the value pattern.

Scott's Square, **embellished, black and white** This black and white photo shows the new value pattern.

Scott's Square is shown here in black and white. I decided to try to lower the contrast in values, so the yellow and orange pieces wouldn't be so bright. I added a lot of texture and color with stitching and added darker values with paint and glitter: thus, *Scott's Square*, embellished. The result of the changes I made to the values of the colors shows in *Scott's Square*, embellished, black and white. The value changes are subtle but definitely soften the contrasts between the pieces.

Options

1. Do the same on a set of blocks or a small quilt top you have already finished.

2. Do the same to a quilt you have already quilted! Make a photocopy of a photograph of the quilt to compare value patterns.

Scott's Square, **embellished** To lower the contrast in values and detract from the brightness of the yellow and orange pieces, I added texture and color with stitching, paint, and glitter.

Color Wheel in Spools Organize the spools and skeins into a color wheel, with primary colors, secondary colors, and tertiary colors in their correct positions.

Color Project

Take all your threads off their racks and out of their boxes and bowls. If that would take a moving van, just pick one of each color to do this. Organize the spools (and skeins) into a color wheel, with primary colors, secondary colors, and tertiary colors in their correct positions. Put the duller colors inside the circle and the dark grays, browns, and blacks in the center, as they are in Color Triangle (see page 61). In what part of the color triangle do you have the most colors? In which part the least? Do you have mostly primary and secondary colors? Or do you have mostly dull, neutral colors in the center? I did this with some of my thread and this was the result: Color Wheel in Spools.

Options

1. Try the same with swatches of fabric. Use as many as possible to get a good sample. Ask yourself the same questions about your fabrics as with your threads.
2. Make your own color wheel with fabric. Cut the pieces and glue them to paper or fuse them to fabric.

Pattern Project

Look through all your fabric and find the two pieces that are most different in type and scale of pattern (ignore the colors). Combine these with solid-colored fabric to make a block. Observe how the scale and type of pattern influence the focal point of the block. I made two blocks to see what would happen: in both *X Print* and *X Solid*, the print dominates the design, partly because it is light colored but mostly because it is large scale with high contrast.

Option

Make a second block with the opposite arrangement of solids and patterns. How does the change impact the design? Which do you like best? Do you want to make more of each to make a small quilt top?

X Print Observe how the scale and type of pattern influence the focal point of the block.

X Solid The print dominates this design, partly because it is light colored but mostly because it has a large scale with high contrast.

Texture Project

Cut an 18″ square of fabric, any solid or mostly solid color. Use pins to baste it to an 18″ square of batting and then to a backing. Use a chalk pencil or a marker that will disappear to divide the square into 8 to 12 spaces, all the same shape, or all different shapes. Use stitching to make a different texture in each shape. Use threads close to the color of the fabric so you can focus on texture. Remember that hand and machine stitches will give different textures and so will variations in the thickness of the thread, the density of the stitching, and the pattern in the stitching. *Blue Texture* uses a heavy machine satin stitch in a diagonal curved line across the block. The other stitches were made both with machine and hand quilting in different patterns that created considerably different textures. I used two sizes (30 and 50) mercerized cotton thread, which only shows up at close range.

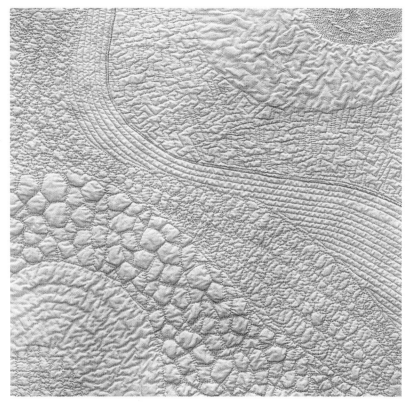

Blue Texture This block uses hand and machine quilting and two thread sizes.

Options

1. Use threads of any color for the stitching.
2. Use textured or patterned fabrics to begin with.
3. Use your couching foot with various yarns and textured threads.

ASK QUESTIONS CONTINUOUSLY

Each quilt you make could be designed in a completely different way. When do you ask the questions? The question-asking process is a problem-solving process, and each quilt presents different questions. I have designed quilts in all of the following ways: plan it all in advance, lines, shapes, and textures, do all the work, then ask questions; pick a starting place and start, asking questions as I work, step by step; plan nothing at all and change my mind as I see what actually happens.

Line, shape, value, color, texture, and pattern are elements for you to use to make your quilt the way you want it to be. They can be arranged, repeated, and changed to create the design that makes the impact or effect you want. One of the last questions to ask is, of course, does it say what you want it to say? It may mean different things to different people, so the question is, does it say to you what you want it to say?

Sunset Strips 5 49" × 31", 1998.

9

❖ ❖ ❖

One Quiltmaker's Decisions

I thought it might help if I described some of the decisions I have made for different quilts along the way. I can describe some of my decision-making methods and how they have evolved. I don't always make decisions the same way on every quilt. I don't always ask the same questions. In fact, the entire way I make decisions has been evolving over the years. And one quilt leads me on to new ideas and more new quilts, many of which remain unmade or unfinished. It seems, looking back on my quilts, that most of them were made so I could find out the answer to a question: what would happen to this quilt if I . . . ? I usually had a goal, to try something or several things, to see what would happen to the design.

AN EVOLUTION

My first quilts were traditional pieced and appliqué quilts. The design was predetermined; I just picked out the colors and patterns and adjusted the size. Then sometimes I planned my own border and picked out a quilting pattern that I liked to fill in the shapes of the design. I often planned all this out before the first piece was cut. Gradually, I started changing the traditional quilt designs a little bit, combining blocks that I hadn't seen together, and I started learning to draw my own quilting lines to fit the quilt top. At first I drew them on paper and traced them onto the quilt. Later, I drew them directly on the quilt top, freehand with chalk pencils so I could change my mind.

After making many traditional quilts, I began to use them instead as inspiration for a design that was my own. My *Birds in Flight* series (see page 28) started this way. When I planned *Granddaughter's Fan*, I wanted to know how different colors would look when they overlapped using the transparent colors of dye. I also wanted to know how four small quarter fans would fit together in a circle. How would the painted edges look different from pieced edges if I quilted in between the colors?

These painted quilts were preplanned and drawn on paper first, but I couldn't plan the quilting until the top was completely ready. As I became more adept at painting the dyes, I was able to create more realistic images in my quilt tops and often avoided piecing and appliqué altogether. In *Flying Ferns*, I wanted to know

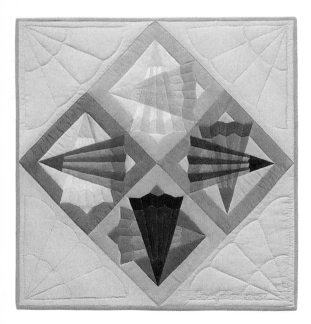

Granddaughter's Fan 23" × 23", 1987. How would different colors look when overlapped, using the transparent colors of dye?

Flying Ferns 30" × 33", 1988. How would a portion of the image look in white only? I painted the center and drew the continuation of the shapes into the border using quilting stitches.

how part of the image would look in white only. I painted the center and drew the continuation of the shapes into the border using quilting stitches. The problem became one of visual impact. In the center of the quilt, I had to find a way to accentuate the shapes without distracting from the image underneath; in the white border, I wanted to create shapes with just texture and pattern.

I eventually stopped painting whole-cloth quilts and started cutting up some of my painted images, using them to piece and appliqué into quilt tops. I usually had an idea of how I wanted the quilt to look by having a sketch on paper, but I was beginning to realize that I should make decisions along the way. I had to do one step before I would know what to do next. As planning ahead became more difficult, the whole process of making a quilt became more exciting, because there were many choices to make as the quilt progressed.

In my first *Merry-Go-Round* quilt, I painted the horses on

Merry-Go-Round 62" × 52", 1990. This quilt uses many techniques: dye painting, machine piecing, hand appliqué, metallic paints, beading, machine and hand quilting. The planning process for making a quilt can be open-ended.

one piece of silk, then hung it on the wall for four or five months because I wanted more texture in the background than painting would give. I wanted more of the look of a quilt, having layers or seams. I decided I wanted a curved, golden wood floor under the horses, but I really didn't want to draw templates and seam allowances to piece it. So I laid the silk on the cutting board, eyeballed the curves, and cut, sewing each seam and ironing it before cutting the next curve. I had to teach myself a new process before I could finish the quilt. I appliquéd the horses and then had to plan a design to quilt. For me, *Merry-Go-Round* was the beginning of realizing how open-ended the planning process could be. I tried techniques on that quilt that I had never done before, like using acrylic paint on the silk, gluing rhinestones, and combining machine and hand quilting. I made many quilts in the next few years that were preplanned to various degrees, but the freedom of planning as the quilt develops is irresistible.

People Tester This is the patch I used to test my quilting and later painted over the figures to see if I wanted to paint on the quilt.

Now, eight years later, I have gone to the other extreme. I often start a quilt with no idea how it will look when I am done. I have realized that a quilt is not necessarily done even when it is all quilted and bound. After *Sunset Strips 5* was quilted, I decided it needed a lot more gold. Adding a few horizontal lines of shiny gold thread wasn't enough (see page 100). In order to try a few options before working on the actual quilt, I used the swatch of fabric and batting I had used for auditioning thread colors and for adjusting my machine tension to test various gold threads and gold paints. As I painted and stitched on Gold Tester, I realized how critical the patterns are that I use to apply the gold paint and thread. I decided to use paint because I wanted heavy gold, and heavy stitching flattens the parts I stitch too much. As I tested different gold paints, I also tried different patterns. I ended up putting a lot of gold on *Sunset Strips 5*.

Sometimes a quilt *is* done, after all. When *Balancing Act 7* (see page 36) was finished, I thought about painting in the figures to make them show up more. I used the sample I had used for quilting tension, People Tester, to see how it would look. I tried a few different colors and brushstrokes, then decided I liked the figures' ambiguity the way they were.

HOW ONE QUILT LEADS TO ANOTHER

Artists mean different things when they talk about working in a series. They may mean that the quilts vary, but actually look somewhat similar, or they may mean that the quilts are related in one or a few details, but that they look different. What I mean is that the idea behind the quilts is related, that making one quilt has led me to making the next, and that they share a concept I am pursuing. To give an idea of how you might let one idea lead to another in your quiltmaking, I will describe one series of quilts I have been developing over the last seven years.

Crazy quilts started me off in 1991 on a series that I have come to refer to as my "step quilts." I set myself the task of making a small silk baby quilt, piecing it the way I thought crazy quilts were pieced—no pattern, no color scheme in

Gold Tester I tested different gold paints and threads; at the same time, I also tried different patterns.

mind. I found it difficult to be random, so I limited myself to what was actually in my scrap box. The finished blocks were too random for me, so I used a solid sashing to assemble them; I placed the blocks so that the red pieces in them formed a diagonal step pattern from one corner of the quilt to the other, like the

Stairway at Zion The contrast of the carved stairway with the curvilinear lines in the rock is heightened by the value difference in the top and bottom halves of the photo. Photograph by the author.

carved stairway in a rock wall in Zion National Park, shown here in Stairway at Zion. My title, *Elements of Stile*, refers to the word that means steps used to get over a fence. The reference to stile reminded me of seeing Inca walls with stones jutting out so a person could climb from one terrace to the next without having to walk all the way around to the actual stairway, shown in Inca Wall. In order to add a layer of complexity and mystery to *Elements of Stile*, I machine quilted the universally used ancient volute design over the blocks, then painted gray dye in those shapes. I also painted stripes on the blue, not liking the solid look the sashing had. My crazy quilt

Inca Wall The terraces look like a large-scale stairway, giving a sense of the size and steepness of the terrain at Puyupatmarca, ruins on the Inca Trail. In the center of the photograph, stones that jut out from each terrace wall are visible. They provide a way to climb from one level to the next. Photograph by the author.

had become a step quilt, and it had become the first in a series that I hadn't planned to start. Two of the questions I wanted to answer while making *Elements of Stile* were about making new shapes with quilting lines that overlapped the piecing shapes, and about the impact of the image of steps, barely suggested by the red lines in the quilt and referred to in the title.

Elements of Stile 31″ × 32″, 1991. How much would the red steps show up after I quilted and painted new shapes over the pieced background?

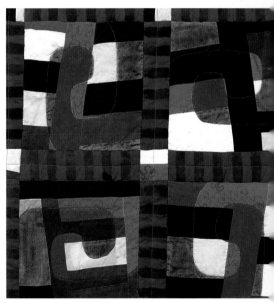

Elements of Stile, **detail** I machine quilted the ancient volute design over the blocks, then painted gray dye in those shapes and painted stripes over the solid blue sashing.

My next step quilt, #2, started in 1992, progressed from scraps to blocks to a small pieced quilt top, then to an over-dyed quilt top, to curved strips (cut up again), and to partly pieced again. It is now in a bag of scraps that I gave away this year. It wasn't answering any questions.

I began using a computer paint program in 1992 to explore the possibilities of the hexagon. I came up with several designs I wanted to make into quilts. I made *Red Flags* (see page 54) in part to answer questions about how to make nonobjective shapes and how the repetition of those shapes makes them into new ones. I liked the irregular, curved line of red shapes, the sets of steps and truncated pyramids floating in the background. When it was quilted, I thought it needed a little more depth, so I painted shadows in behind the red shapes. That's when I lost the nonobjectivity and they became stiff red flags to me.

The design for *Steps 4* came from the same computer work with hexagons, but it started to look more like steps than *Red Flags*. It interested me because of the shaded pyramid shapes. By the time I painted and dyed all the fabric for this quilt and pieced it, I was beginning to do more free-motion quilting. This quilt provided the problem of how to add machine quilting designs that enhanced the quilt top without taking away from the impact of the shapes.

Steps 4 67" × 54", 1994. I wondered how to plan quilting that would add detail without distracting from the painted and pieced shapes. Similarly, for *Steps 5, Lightning* (see page 44) I wondered if I could piece lightning in a jagged line across the quilt like steps.

In 1995 I took a workshop from Nancy Crow and learned techniques and approaches to designing that enable me to plan a quilt without worrying about how to piece it. When I made *Steps 5, Lightning* (see page 44), I wanted to experiment with my new skills and I wanted to see how I could suggest stairs with blocks and lines. I wanted to put pieced lines in my quilts that looked like lines, instead of creating shapes with them. I put the crazy-pieced blocks together with angular gold lines of lightning moving from top to bottom.

Balancing Act I, *II*, and *III* are quilt designs in which the main element is line. In all three, the lines make a structure with stepped sides like a pyramid, but each is an uneven and insubstantial pyramid that may not remain standing. Making *Balancing Act I* (see page 2), I practiced learning to draw lines with piecing. In *Balancing Act II* (see page 10), I wanted to know how it would look if the lines had more exaggerated curves. I had no idea at all what the whole effect would be if I used a realistic image like the baby feet as a repeat design element. Using a combination of hand and machine quilting allowed me to change what would happen to the design by adding texture and pattern to the surface of the quilt. I started a little piece while I was making *Balancing Act II* to try different piecing arrangements and to audition different threads and quilting stitches. I called it *Balancing Act 4* (see page ii) because I finished it after number *III*.

When I was ready to start *Balancing Act III* (see page 11), I wanted to make an all-gold quilt, so I reversed the values of the line and the background from the other two quilts. I decided to use strong, smooth pieced lines to contrast with the thin, irregular lines in the gold fabric and use that fabric to give a variety of line directions. I wanted to see how amorphous quilting lines would contrast with the structural pieced and painted lines.

I wanted to make *Balancing Act 5 (Ladder)* (see page 42) an interesting design without bright colors, with more emphasis on value contrast. I wondered how my stepped structure built of lines would be affected by a strong design in the background fabric. As I thought about piecing in the long light horizontal line at the bottom of the structure to hold it all up, I realized that the balance of the whole composition was much better with the line floating at the top, so that's where I put it.

By the time I started *Caution, Construction Zone* (see page 56) I had gotten into a rhythm of cutting and assembling fabric that I really like. In this quilt, I decided to make a ladder central to the design. I wanted to try using fabric with a strong pattern and distinct lines. As I put it together, I felt like I was building a structure, trying to make it balance.

I had an image with big, curved stairs in my mind when I started *North Is Up* (see page 1) and I wanted to see what I could do, starting with the stair shapes cut out freehand with no pattern. The rest of the quilt and the questions came along after I placed the gold stairs on the wall. The ideas I worked on as I made this quilt were how to create a sense of space, how to give a suggestion of maps, and what technique to use to put the people on the stairs.

After I put people in *North Is Up*, I wanted to use people on my next quilt, but this time making them more visible. The question with *Balancing Act 7* (see page 36) was, could I resolve the themes of balancing, structures, and stairways using the fabric I wanted to use with a semicircular shape repeated all over it? I wondered how to give the people's activities a sense of mystery and where and how to build the stair structure for the balancing act.

The scraps from another quilt became *Balancing Act 8* (see page 120). No people, no stairs, but the same pyramid shape and the same problem of balance got me involved and puts this quilt in direct succession in this series. Most of my questions on this quilt concerned how to use value and texture to add dimension to the design.

I went back to the ladder image in *Balancing Act 9* (see page 70). The stair structure is cut off at the top to become a balance beam. In this quilt I was questioning foreground and background, which colors come forward or recede, and where to use patterned fabric.

One quilt led to another, even though the methods were decided along the way. Even as I pieced the grid on the background of *North Is Up*, I realized that it was the beginning of another series—sketch maps. As I write this, I have only completed *North Is Up*, but I have started, sketched, and/or selected fabric for five more quilts in my sketch map series. One of them is the mate to *North Is Up*.

Balancing Act 9, **detail** In this quilt I wanted to see how the bright green background would balance with the dark red foreground, and at what point it would become foreground.

Double Stair This is a quick sketch I made so I would remember my idea for a spiral stair quilt.

ONE QUILT'S PROGRESS

North Is Up began as a sketch I made while not listening to a lecture in 1993, Double Stair. I had taken photographs of some circular stairways in my travels and wanted to pursue the image in my quilts: Museum Stairway and Castle Stairway had the spiral effect that I liked. I played with the idea on the computer, producing spiral designs, such as Computer Sketch. It took a while to start, though, because I couldn't decide how to treat perspective and scale and how I would construct it. I sketched more stairs, deciding on a single spiral: Single Stair Sketch. I had eliminated the double stairway concept and had decided to do a pair of quilts.

In 1997, I picked one of my favorite pieces of gold fabric and cut out the shapes freehand, putting them each on the wall to see how to cut the next one. The golden stairway was arranged on my flannel wall, waiting for me to decide what to do next. During the time that I was choosing fabrics for the background I ran into one that reminded me of contour lines on a map. I decided to follow that train of thought while the stairs waited. To get the idea down quickly, I cut

Museum Stairway Photos of this spiral stairway taken from several angles helped me to decide how I might design a spiral stair in fabric. Photograph by the author.

Castle Stairway I liked the spiral effect of this stone ramp in a castle in Germany, so I added it to my wall of ideas for the quilt I was planning. Photograph by the author.

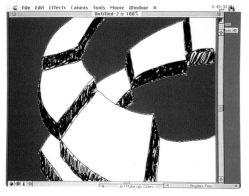

Computer Sketch I used my computer paint program to draw and redraw spiral designs as practice for a quilt I would eventually make.

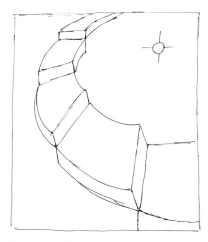

Single Stair Sketch This is the sketch I made to plan the simplified quilt idea.

Sketch Map I Instead of sketching on paper to work out an idea, I may cut fabric and fuse it to another piece of fabric.

shapes to represent scale of miles and other typical map symbols, then applied them to a small piece of that same fabric. I had Sketch Map I and, at the same time, I realized that what I needed for the background of my gold stairs was longitude and latitude lines. The rest followed logically: a north arrow, the title *North Is Up*, and the people on the stairway going in every direction.

I can show you how its companion piece progressed. First I decided the new quilt would not necessarily be like *North Is Up*, because it would answer new questions, to be determined along the way. I decided it would be the southern hemisphere, so I constructed the stairway in bright green for *Green Stairs* (see page 110), going the opposite direction; this time I used patterned fabric for the risers and shadows. I put up many fabrics before I chose the intense red for the background; the light blue fabric I found on my shelf looked like it should be the polar ice cap for Background Added (see page 110). The linear designs on the tan/brown fabric looked like settlement patterns and I realized I wanted the ice to look like swirling clouds, turning counterclockwise, as they do in the southern hemisphere. In Background Changed (see page 110), I had placed some of the tan/brown fabric. Then I turned some of the light blue fabric to accentuate the swirl to the left and painted on silver latitude and longitude lines. By the time I

Green Stairs The second spiral stair quilt would answer new questions. I constructed the stairway going the opposite direction, using patterned fabric for the risers and shadows.

Background Added I first chose an intense red fabric with strong dark blue marks for the background. The light blue fabric I found on my shelf was perfect for the polar ice cap or clouds.

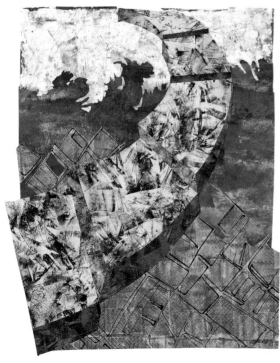

Background Changed I added a tan/brown fabric with linear designs to be my "civilization."

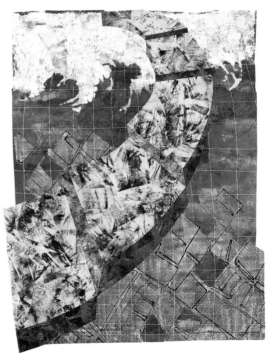

Coriolis Effect, quilt top The quilt top has surface stitching, reverse appliqué, and silver paint added for texture and detail. I still planned to add a directional arrow, but couldn't decide how I would do it.

Coriolis Effect, **detail** The cold front is indicated by a couched blue ribbon and three-dimensional triangles. It overlaps the silver latitude and longitude lines and the black contour lines of the pressure zones as well as the appliqué design of the landscape below.

had a finished quilt top, it had a name. As a quilt top, *Coriolis Effect* had surface stitching, direct and reverse appliqué, and silver paint added for texture and detail. I started by stitching the people on the stairway in heavy red thread. Then I added high and low pressure contour lines with heavy black thread. Seeing that they didn't show up very much, I thickened the lines with black paint. Zigzag stitching over the silver longitude and latitude lines gave them some dimension and emphasized them even more. I fused and stitched the compass onto the lower right corner and, as the last step, couched the blue and red ribbons, triangles, and half circles to represent cold and warm fronts. I decided to leave the edge irregular, in keeping with my idea that the quilt is a part of something larger. The finished quilt is shown on page 85.

One Block One of the original pieced blocks for *Gold Sketch Map*.

Four Blocks Painted Four of the blocks assembled, then dyed again.

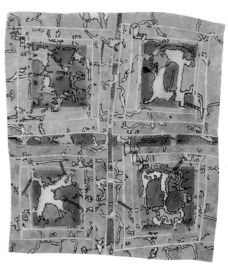

***Four Blocks,* back** The wrong side of the four blocks after dye painting; the seams are lighter because the color didn't penetrate through all layers.

THERE IS NO END

When *Coriolis Effect* was done, I could finish the quilt I pieced three years ago when I wanted to make a gold quilt. It turns out that it's a sketch map, too. *One Block* shows a detail of the original fabric color and the piecing. *Four Blocks Painted* shows the quilt after I pieced four blocks together then painted in black lines and various colors of tan and gold around the lines. The back of *Four Blocks* shows how the back looked after it was painted; the seams contrast in value with the rest because the color I painted on the front didn't penetrate through their thickness. That extra interest of the contrast made me decide to use the back as the front. I machine stitched contour lines all around the shapes with variegated thread and used heavy black thread on the ladders and stairs to give them emphasis: *Gold Sketch Map* is the result.

Gold Sketch Map 28" × 26", 1998. Machine stitching with variegated thread and heavy black thread added even more texture to the quilt design.

Meanwhile, I am hustling along to make another new sketch map quilt I saw in a piece of fabric that I dyed recently, Four Quarters. I wanted to represent the intersection of the four quarters of the world in the Inca cosmology, so this quilt became an imaginary map based on an idea, not a place. I made a sketch and notes about what I would do first and what I might consider next. I did the first step I planned, which was to add a heavy dark crossroads to the design: *Tawantinsuyo*, in progress. Then I embroidered orange lines in the shapes of stones over the black appliqué to integrate them more with the ground fabric. By the time I was ready to go on with the next step I had planned, I had a new idea. I decided to cut a trapezoidal window in each quarter to show two more layers of pattern—one adapted from Inca weavings and, beneath that, one suggesting the designs found on the coastal desert of Peru—to reflect layers of culture. This time, even though I had planned in advance with notes and sketches, the design continued to change as I worked on the quilt, *Tawantinsuyo*.

Now it might be time to go back and finish Sketch Map 1 (see page 109). The point is that the choices are many and time is short! I make quilts with the attitude that it will be a learning process. I think I may actually work on Sketch Map 1 because my current plans for it include techniques I want to practice, such as creating contour lines with machine embroidery on a single layer of starched fabric, and couching my hand-dyed pearl cotton in a grid. I want to try having the front look like an inset from another map—which will be on the back of the quilt—and coordinate the quilting lines to go with both sides. Maybe I'll get to it tomorrow.

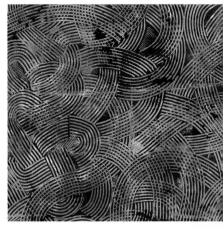

Four Quarters Looking at this fabric gave me an idea for a new quilt design.

Tawantinsuyo, **in progress, detail** My first step was to add a heavy dark crossroads to the design.

Tawantinsuyo 32" × 45", 1998. The design of this quilt changed completely after the first layer was embroidered.

Night Falls 42" × 52", 1998.

10

♦ ♦ ♦

Starting Places

Where does the idea for a quilt really start? Even the person who makes the quilt may not know the answer. It does help me to look back and figure out sources of ideas because it makes me more aware of where I might get ideas in the future. It makes me ready to see new ideas when they come along. This approach seems to work because I always have so many ideas for quilts that I have to choose among them when I am ready to start a new one. As soon as I see them or think of them, they go up on My Idea Wall in the workroom. I have enough notes, hints, pictures, and sketches of ideas and things to try that sometimes I don't get around to an idea for several years.

My Idea Wall I have a big mess of ideas, new and old, on a wall in my workroom.

WHERE DID I START?

Where did I start when I made *Night Falls*? I think its origins are in earlier quilts. My first rock quilt was *Rolling Stone* in 1987, inspired by the traditional block of the same name. I wanted to use the quilt pattern to suggest a progression from a hot day to cool evening, from earth to sky, from bottom to top. I started with paper and pencil, drawing the same block repeated 25 times. I copied it several times and filled in different designs with colored pencils.

In 1989, I decided I wanted to play with the concept of a garden made of rock, so during that year and the next, I made *Rock Garden I*, *Rock Garden II: Latourelle Falls*, and *Rock Garden III: Paint Brush*. They were all designed directly from photographs of rocks and plants. In *Rock Garden I*, I was working on abstracting the image and combin-

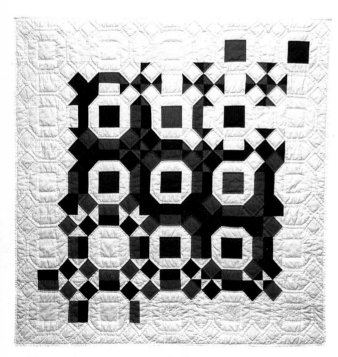

Rolling Stone 44" × 44", 1987. Hand quilted by Dorothy Campbell. I wanted to use the traditional quilt pattern to suggest a progression from a hot day to cool evening, from earth to sky, from bottom to top. Photograph by the author.

Rock Garden I 39" × 37", 1989. Hand quilted by Diane Roberts. This quilt was inspired by a photo I saw of a pile of rocks with a few tall grasses.

ing appliqué and piecing. In *Latourelle Falls* and *Paint Brush*, I worked from my photographs and tried to reproduce selected parts of the image as exactly as I could, using dye painting and hand quilting. I took the Basalt Columns photo at Latourelle Falls along the Columbia Gorge; the columns really do look like they are upside down.

Rock Garden III: Paint Brush 49" × 41", 1989. I made this small quilt to see what I could do with the texture of granite and a delicate flower shape.

Rock Garden II: Latourelle Falls 49" × 41", 1989. I was challenged to make a quilt by one of the awesome places in the Columbia Gorge where the water undercuts the rock. The problem was how to use hand quilting to enhance the detail I could paint on the silk.

Basalt Columns I worked from this photo to get the details right when I drew the lines and dye painted the quilt top. Photograph by the author.

I wanted to try working more abstractly, so I decided to piece *Vermilion Cliffs*, inspired by our visit to Bryce Canyon and the Grand Canyon, instead of painting it. It was a full year between the time I created the design and when I realized that I had all the colors on my shelf and started piecing. By the time I made my next rock quilt, I had become more interested in simplifying and making abstract shapes from my ideas. *#146, Rock Garden IV* is a painted abstraction from the idea of rocks. First I dyed the fabric and, later, looking at it made me think of cracked rocks and rock walls, so I dyed it again to accentuate the shapes that were suggested in the first layer of color, then machine quilted it to give it even more dimension.

Vermilion Cliffs 60″ × 82″, 1993. This quilt is a pieced abstraction of Bryce Canyon.

#146, Rock Garden IV 57″ × 39″, 1994. The dyed fabric came first, then the idea of a rock wall. I dyed the fabric again to make more shadows, and quilted it for texture.

The idea of *Night Falls* also began with a particular piece of fabric, Nighttime Blue. It was one of those fabrics that accidentally came out great when I dyed it. I didn't know what I wanted to do with it, so I waited. I took a picture of it and scanned it into my computer. Eventually, using a computer paint program, I arranged and rearranged the rock/crystal images suggested in the fabric by "cutting out parts" and "pasting" them into a blank background. I had lots of variations of Blue Rocks before I was done. In order to fill the background, I picked up the image of the whole piece of fab-

Nighttime Blue I liked this fabric too much to cut it up, so I took a picture of it.

ric, enlarged, with my "copy" tool and inserted it behind the rock shapes. It wasn't very interesting until I rotated the background so that the dark rocks were in front of the light parts of the fabric. Then it became an idea ready to become a quilt, Falling Rocks.

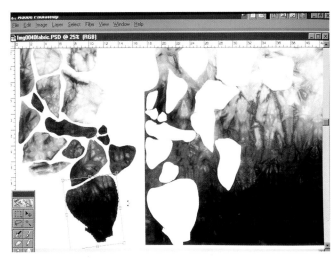

Blue Rocks Using my computer program, I could arrange and rearrange the rock/crystal images suggested in the fabric by "cutting out parts" and "pasting" them into a blank background.

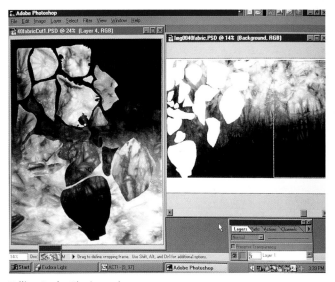

Falling Rocks The image became more interesting to me after I turned the background image 180° to create more value contrast.

Glacial Deposit Huge rocks can perch precariously. The idea has gotten into my quilts. Photograph by the author.

As I cut the shapes out of the real fabric, I decided I wanted smooth edges like river rocks, rather than rough edges as I had in my computer image. I cut out the shapes behind the appliqué and used some of them on the front. I reshaped the smaller pieces and by the time I had arranged another piece of fabric on them, in order to practice embroidery stitches I would use on *Night Falls*, I had another quilt design. I piled the shapes up like rocks in a stone cairn and at the last minute took one out of the middle, leaving another barely balancing pyramid, *Balancing Act 8*. It reminded me of some of the ways rocks perch precariously in the mountains, as in the photo Glacial Deposit. After hours of stitching and miles of thread, I had only partly embroidered both quilt tops. I had a long way to go because I wanted to have lots and lots of texture. I began to change my mind: maybe I didn't want all that texture on "smooth" rocks; maybe the texture would go in the background. And how do I enhance the theme of night? Stars! The last step on *Night Falls*, after it was bound, was putting on falling streaks of dark glitter.

Balancing Act 8 25" × 25", 1998. Moving the pieces of fabric shaped like river rocks around on a background gave me many options for designs. I liked it best after taking one out of the middle, leaving a barely balancing pyramid.

BEFORE YOU START

Analyze How You Design

Be aware of how *you* begin making a new quilt. Think about the answers you have to these questions and consider your approach to designing.

- Do you try several ways of designing before you really start?
- Do you determine how the quilt will look before you start?
- Do you know how you will construct the quilt before you start?
- Do you ever change your mind about the design of the quilt after you start?
- Do you ever seek out information about a technique you have never tried in order to make a certain quilt?
- Do you pick all the fabrics for a quilt before you start?

Try this step-by-step process to help you determine the way you approach designing.

Step one: Pick three or more subjects from the following list, or choose three subjects of your own, making them as specific as possible.

Subjects
thorny red roses
triangles in motion
mountains with snow
friendship that ends
fear of heights
dead ferns
sand dunes
bats hanging upside down
apartment houses
wedding cake
speeding cars
cloud forest
anger at loss
Other _____

Step two: Decide how you would approach the chosen subjects to begin a quilt. What is the *first* thing you would do? Write down each subject you have chosen with a starting place from the following list, or add options to the list.

Starting Places
Make a small drawing to scale
Make a drawing of the full-size design
Cut without a plan, with/without rulers, fabric already chosen
Look for a traditional pattern in your quilt resources
Use your computer design software
Use your computer paint or drawing software

Choose a photograph from your collection to use as a design
Paint on paper
Paint on fabric
Sort all your fabric, looking for a piece that goes with the subject
Look in your idea notebooks or your bulletin board of ideas
Other _____

Step three: Think about your choices.

- Does the subject have anything to do with your starting place?
- Are all the starting places the same?
- What is your favorite way to start?
- Do you want to try new ways to start?

Analyze How You Build a Quilt
Be aware that the techniques you choose to construct and finish your quilt will have a huge influence on how it looks when you are done. Ask yourself the following questions.

1. Which of these *construction* techniques do you use?

	ALWAYS	SOMETIMES	NEVER
Straight-edge piecing	—	—	—
Curved piecing with templates or patterns	—	—	—
Freehand curve piecing	—	—	—
Raw-edge fused appliqué	—	—	—
Blind-stitch appliqué, turned-under edges	—	—	—
Reverse appliqué	—	—	—
Whole cloth, hand-painted design	—	—	—
Other _____	—	—	—

2. Do you ever use two or more of the above in the same quilt?
3. Which do you use the most often? Why?

1. Which of these *quilting* techniques do you use?

	ALWAYS	SOMETIMES	NEVER
Machine, free-motion	—	—	—
Machine, walking foot	—	—	—
Hand quilting, small stitches	—	—	—
Hand quilting, varied size stitches	—	—	—
One color quilting thread	—	—	—
Varied color quilting threads	—	—	—
Other _____	—	—	—

2. Do you ever use two or more of the above in the same quilt?
3. Which do you use the most often? Why?

1. Which of these *embellishment* techniques do you use?

	ALWAYS	SOMETIMES	NEVER
Beading, buttons, charms	—	—	—
Glitter glue	—	—	—
Fabric paint	—	—	—
Couched decorative threads	—	—	—
Satin-stitch machine embroidery	—	—	—
Free-motion zigzag embroidery	—	—	—
Hand embroidery	—	—	—
Trims, ribbon, lace	—	—	—
None of the above	—	—	—
Other _____	—	—	—

2. Do you ever use two or more of the above in the same quilt?
3. Which do you use the most often? Why?

Think about your answers. Do you need to try different techniques to achieve the design you want? The same design can look entirely different if other techniques are used. Making quilts is most exciting when you can decide which construction/quilting/embroidery techniques work best for how you want your design to look. I made sketches and took photographs while I was in the Wallowa Mountains. Cracked Rock is a photo of a place I sketched in Lines in Stone. From this sketch, I made a pieced block, *Pieced Stones*; a fused appliqué block, *Fused Stones*; and a painted block, *Painted Stones*, to see what I could do with each technique (see page 124). The subject, shapes, and colors are the same, but the technique used has made a big difference in the appearance of the final blocks.

Cracked Rock When I was in the Wallowa Mountains, I was surrounded by shapes that provided new quilt ideas. Photograph by the author.

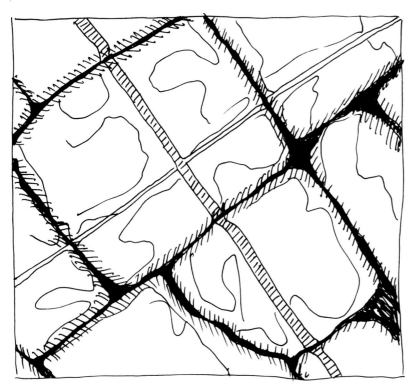

Lines in Stone Line drawings eliminate the colors and simplify the shapes to help make the design for a block.

Pieced Stones Piecing creates smooth lines around the shapes, simplifying them even more.

Painted Stones Paint can add any amount of color, any amount of detail. I used shading with black lines here to give some dimension to the shapes.

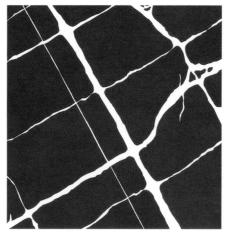

Fused Stones Fusing fabric has the potential for complex and detailed shapes.

FIVE PLACES TO START

These projects are designed to start you thinking about quilt design in ways you might not have tried before. They may lead you to a design, but I do not intend them to end in patterns for specific quilts. When you are concentrating on design, don't focus on how you will put the quilt together, but rather on how to make the design work the way you want it to.

Play with a Traditional Pattern

Find a simple traditional quilt pattern that uses repeating blocks, such as *Spool*, *Fence Rail*, or *Pin Wheel*. Use paper with a grid on it and draw the lines of the block, repeating 12 times: 4 across and 5 down. Shortcuts involve using a copier or a computer to get the pattern on paper, as in the Rolling Stone line drawing. Then make at least four black and white copies so you have the whole quilt design, blank, on four pieces of paper. Color them four completely different ways. Ignore the divisions between the blocks. Use felt pens, colored pencils, crayons, watercolor pencils, paint, or use your computer to fill in the colors.

Remember to focus on the arrangement of the colors, not on what media you are using. The point is to try things you would not bother to do if you had to cut the fabric, sew the pieces, and iron the seams! Keep in mind that the design started with a repeat block, but you do not need to use the edges of the block as line elements of your design—see the color versions of Rolling Stone.

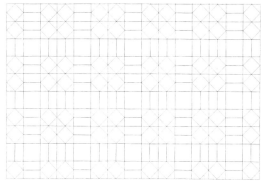

Rolling Stone drawing The traditional block is repeated here multiple times.

Rolling Stone in color Filling in colors on the whole blank pattern allows an infinite number of designs from the same basic quilt pattern. Here are four possibilities.

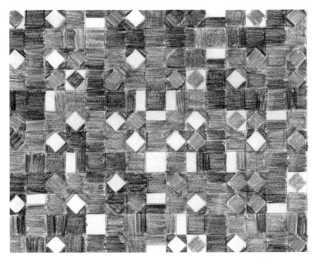

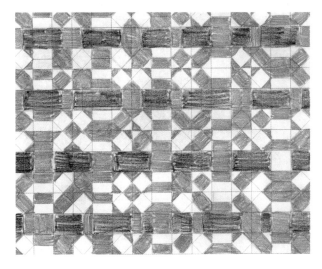

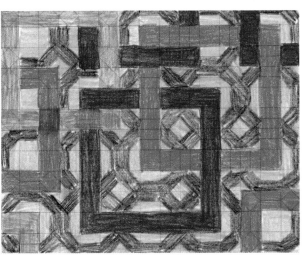

Six Big Blocks These six blocks are the starting place for all the samples that follow.

Cut Fabric Without a Template

The focus of this project is discovery: how the lines and shapes you cut work together. Assemble six to eight 12″ to 18″ blocks. Keep the color combinations simple, but be sure you have value contrast, light and dark. I used horizontal blue and white strips. You may wish to use a four patch, diagonal strips, or another simple piecing arrangement. *Six Big Blocks* are the starting place for all the samples that follow. In fact, the four all-blue-and-white blocks in this photo were the starting blocks for *Tod's Quilt* (see page 35). I used the same approach in making that quilt, but as I pieced, I added small chunks of red because I realized I didn't want only blue and white.

Stack the blocks you have made, and cut through them all at once, at least two times but no more than six times. You may wish to use a straight cut, but a gently curving cut will piece together nicely using a narrow seam. Rearrange the layers of fabric into different blocks, using a large flannel board to audition arrangements. If you wish, glue them to paper or piece them together. Trim the outside edges of the blocks and pick four you like the best to assemble. Tape the paper together or piece them.

The first variation of this exercise was made by cutting the stacked blocks in a "V" shape: *One V*. The eight separate blocks I made with the rearranged pieces are shown in *Eight Vs Separate*. The four assembled blocks are shown in *Four Vs Assembled*. The second variation was cut differently, as shown in *Diagonal Cut*. Eight blocks were used

One V The first variation of this exercise was made by cutting the stacked blocks in a gently curving "V" shape. The pieces are shown after they were cut, but before they were rearranged.

for *Diagonal Cut Assembled*. For the third variation, the stack was cut with two large curves, as in *Crescent Cut*. Nine blocks were put together for *Crescent Cut Assembled*. The fourth variation was cut three times, twice from one corner and once from the other corner, making six pieces, in *Cross Cut*. *Cross Cut Assembled* uses nine blocks.

Imagine the possibilities if I had used different starting blocks. The variables are endless. Try a few.

Eight Vs Separate These are the eight blocks I made with the rearranged pieces, before I assembled any of them.

Four Vs Assembled I selected four of the "V" blocks and pieced them together with slightly curved seams.

Diagonal Cut This shows the cut made for the second variation after the stacks were rearranged.

Diagonal Cut Assembled Eight of the diagonal cut blocks, pieced together.

Crescent Cut The pieces after they were cut for the third variation. A curve like this is not difficult to piece!

Crescent Cut Assembled One of the possible arrangements using the crescent cut variation.

Cross Cut The stack of blocks was cut crosswise three times, making six pieces. They were cut and rearranged, but not stitched, for this photo.

Cross Cut Assembled This layout uses nine of the cross-cut blocks. The possibilities were endless.

Design from a Photograph

The object of the project is to start with one image and end up with another. Pick a photo that you took yourself and that you like a lot. Pick one that has distinct lines and/or shapes in it. Take a minute to determine which are the dominant elements in the photograph. Are there some less important shapes or lines in the photo that interest you? The photo, Guatemalan Garden has great shapes and variety, and would be a good one to try.

Use a black pen to draw a few of the shapes or lines you like very quickly and simply on small pieces of paper, approximately 4″ × 4″. Fill the space. Look at what you have drawn and look again at the photograph. Look for other interesting shapes or lines, and draw more. Remember you are not drawing the picture, you are taking out some of its elements and simplifying them. Fill at least ten pieces of paper. As you progress through the variations, you will start to think of more ways to manipulate them. Here are a few variations to try when you draw from the photograph:

- Make the elements repeat, with more or less space between them
- Move them into a symmetrical or asymmetrical arrangement
- Change the size of the elements
- Pick one of the drawn elements and repeat it
- Pick one of the drawn elements and draw a mirror image next to it

I used a photograph I took in Zunil, Guatemala, of Two Trucks for my Ten Sketches. Keep your lines simple and look for elements that interest you or can make interesting combinations. They will come from unexpected places.

Guatemalan Garden The photo contains distinct shapes and has lots of variety of line, making it a good choice for sketching. Photograph by the author.

Two Trucks I used this photo of a Guatemalan church with two trucks in front for my ten sketches. Photograph by the author.

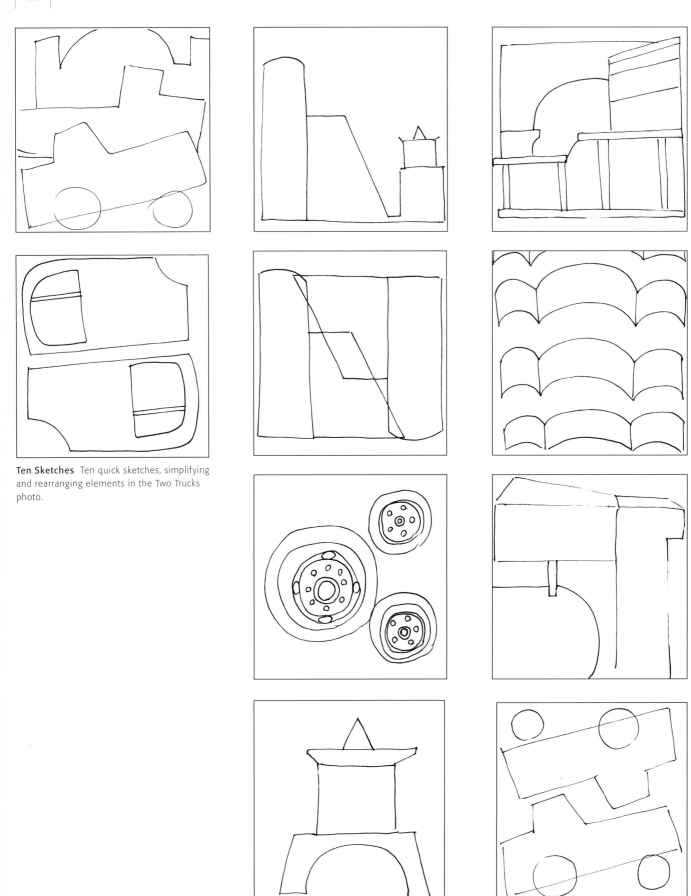

Ten Sketches Ten quick sketches, simplifying and rearranging elements in the Two Trucks photo.

Test Value Patterns

Pick one of your line drawings from the above exercise, or quickly make a few small (4″ × 4″) line drawings and pick one of those. Make four black and white copies of it. Shade the shapes and lines in four completely different value patterns with three to six values of gray, including white and black. Use colored pencils, felt pens, or your computer: Four Value Patterns. Pick your favorite version and enlarge it to 12″ to 16″. Use the large paper drawing as a pattern to cut fabric to fill in the shapes, matching the values. Use grays and black and white or use one color and several different values of that color. Assemble it with glue or fusible web, as in Another Idea.

Four Value Patterns I chose one sketch for testing value patterns.

Another Idea One of the value patterns looks like a good idea when it is cut out of fabric and fused together.

Peruvian Belt, **detail** The motif I chose is on the top row, third from the right.

Find a Motif

Look at textiles from other cultures, anywhere in the world, from any time in history. Use museum catalogs, books in the library, magazines, fabric in your own collection, rugs, weavings. Go to the craft market where you live and look for samples of textiles. Isolate several motifs that have some significance to you or that you particularly like. The motif in *Myers Quilt* (see page 5) is from a knotted rug. I can find several motifs I like in the hand-woven wool belt from Cotabamba, Peru shown in *Peruvian Belt*.

Draw the outline of one of the simpler motifs on paper. Then enlarge the motif to approximately 6″ × 6″ and make several copies. Use one copy to make a pattern for the motif, then cut it out of black or dark colored fabric (with fusible web on the back if you wish), three to eight times. I used the froglike figure in the upper righthand corner of the photograph to create *Frog Motif*. Place the dark shapes on a piece of light fabric and move them around until you find a

Frog Motif One motif, cut from fabric, ready to fuse. The shapes in the background look interesting, too.

Four Frogs Four frogs together create new background shapes.

place where the background shape is as interesting to you as the shape you are working with. You may need to trim the fabric or get a larger piece before you find the arrangement you like best. I ended up with *Four Frogs*—or is it eight?

Another way to work with the motif is to design a background shape that fits one motif, then alternate darks and lights. In order to do this, use a dark fabric motif you have already cut and place it on a light piece of paper. Move it around until you find the background taking shape. Trace the motif in the spot you found and cut the outside edges to the size and shape that fits the motif best. It won't necessarily be a square. Use that piece of paper as a pattern for a background color. So now you have Two Patterns.

Find three or four each, very light fabrics and very dark fabrics. Cut the motif out of each one. You will have six to eight motif shapes, both dark and light. Cut the same number of backgrounds, placing each motif on a background of the opposite value: a light motif on a dark ground, dark motif on a light ground. Assemble by pinning, gluing lightly, or basting so you have six assembled blocks. Move the blocks around on a flannel wall to make a design you like. Use all of them or only some. I cut the motifs in half when I put them across the seams of the pieced background so I could keep the dark and light contrast, as seen in One Layout.

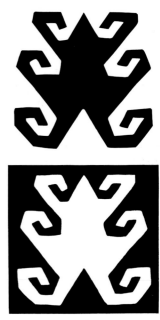

Two Patterns Both paper patterns I used to make background and foreground shapes.

One Layout I cut the motifs in half when I put them across the seams of the pieced background so I could keep the dark and light contrast.

Try it again with the experience you have gained; you may pick a different motif or different colors or values. Remember that you are observing what happens to the shapes, foreground, and background; you are not necessarily making a quilt. The process of using pieces, layered on each other like collage, allows you to look at the design, to test it. You can get a fairly good idea of how it's working without spending a lot of time. It makes it easy to change your mind. The whole project could be done in black and white first, before making the color decisions. As you can see, in this kind of design, color, shape, and value decisions are important considerations.

ONE STEP LEADS TO ANOTHER

One idea leads to many more, like a path in the woods, branching out all over the place! You may start with a traditional quilt pattern, a photograph from your travels, a computer design, a collage of fabrics, an ancient symbol, or a piece of fabric. You may start a new design based on the last quilt you made. The most important thing to start with is an idea. The idea may not be an answer, it may be a question, but it will help you focus your design decisions as you are making the quilt.

The New Development I already know what I want to do with this piece of fabric. It will be a sketch map quilt for sure.

Coriolis Effect and *Tawantinsuyo* are my two most recent quilts, and they have been good practice for my next quilts. I have a great idea for this piece of fabric, The New Development. I can't wait to work with the ideas in this photograph of Tioga Pass. I drew this sketch Snowscape in an airplane six months ago, and now I think I know how I might make a quilt from it. First, I might work on Sketch Map I.

Tioga Pass The shapes and lines in this road grader suggest a quilt to me. Photograph by the author.

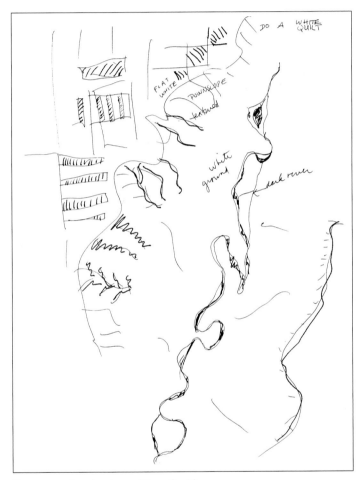

Snowscape I'm planning a white quilt with the shapes of the fields and streams in it, but I don't know how I will make it yet.

❖ ❖ ❖

Definitions

Abstraction: Simplification of natural shapes to essential, basic character.

Arbitrary color: Subjective decision for design, esthetic, or emotional reasons.

Art: Visual solution: Does it communicate the idea? Is it visually effective?

Asymmetrical balance: Dissimilar objects placed with equal visual weight or equal eye attraction.

Balance: Assumes a center vertical axis; we expect to see equal visual weight on either side of that axis. Balance is an equal distribution of visual weight.

Color: That aspect of things that is caused by differing qualities of the light reflected or emitted by them, definable in terms of the observer or of the light. The appearance of objects described in terms of the individual's perception of them, involving hue, lightness, and saturation.

Color discord: Using colors that have no basic affinity for each other, colors widely separated on the color wheel, but not complements.

Color unity: Dominance of a single color or the visual importance of a hue in a whole composition.

Complementary colors: Opposites on the color wheel; opposites in position and character.

Content: Subject, story, or information art seeks to communicate.

Continuation: Planned arrangement of various forms so that their edges are lined up—forms that are "continuous" from one to another within a design.

Contrast: The use of opposing elements, such as colors, value, shape, or lines, in proximity to produce an intensified effect in a work of art. To set in opposition in order to show or emphasize differences.

Crystallographic balance: Allover pattern, equal emphasis over the whole composition.

Curvilinear: Emphasis on curving shapes.

Design: Visual organization, composition.

Focal point: Attracts viewer as a point of emphasis, encourages the viewer to look farther.

Hue: The name of the color. The property of colors by which they can be perceived as ranging from red through yellow, green, and blue, as determined by the dominant wavelength of the light.

Idealization: Presenting the shape as the artist deems it should be.

Implied line: The viewer visually connects the parts of the composition to create a line (continuance).

Intensity: Brightness; full intensity means pure, unmixed colors. Also *chroma, saturation.*

Line: A thin continuous mark; a border or boundary; a contour or an outline. A mark used to define a shape or represent a contour. A line is a shape that has form and width, but it is so narrow compared to its length that width is not the issue.

Linear perspective: As parallel lines recede into the distance, they seem to converge on the horizon.

Mental line: Often the line of sight; we feel a line or a mental connection.

Nonobjective: Use of pure shapes/forms with no reference to any object and no suggestion of a subject matter.

Pattern: A repetitive design in which the motif appears over and over.

Primary colors: Red, yellow, and blue; all other colors are mixed.

Proportion: Relative size measured against other elements or against some mental norm or standard.

Proximity: Closeness of the elements of design.

Radial balance: All the elements radiate out from a common central point.

Realism: The actual appearance of something as it exists in the real world.

Rectilinear: Hard, straight edges and angular corners.

Repetition: An element that repeats in various parts of a design to relate the parts.

Rhythm: In visual art, refers to the movement of the viewer's eye across recurrent motifs.

Shape: A visually perceived area, the edges defined by a line or by color and value changes.

Secondary colors: Mixtures of two primaries; a visual secondary does not always contain equal amounts of the two colors.

Simultaneous contrast: When complements are placed next to each other, colors are intensified.

Symmetrical balance: Shapes, colors, values, or lines repeated on both halves of a composition.

Tertiary colors: Mixtures of a primary and an adjacent secondary.

Texture: The surface tactile quality of objects.

Transformation: Changing the shape to make a point, or emphasize the design.

Unity: Harmony, the quality that makes elements look like they belong together.

Value: Quality of lightness or darkness of a color.

Value pattern: Arrangement and amount of variations in light and dark, independent of color.

Visual texture: What is seen gives the appearance of texture, where actual texture does not exist.

Value: Refers to the darkness or lightness of a color.

Visual color mixing: Two colors side by side in small areas so that the viewer's eye does the mixing (at a certain distance).

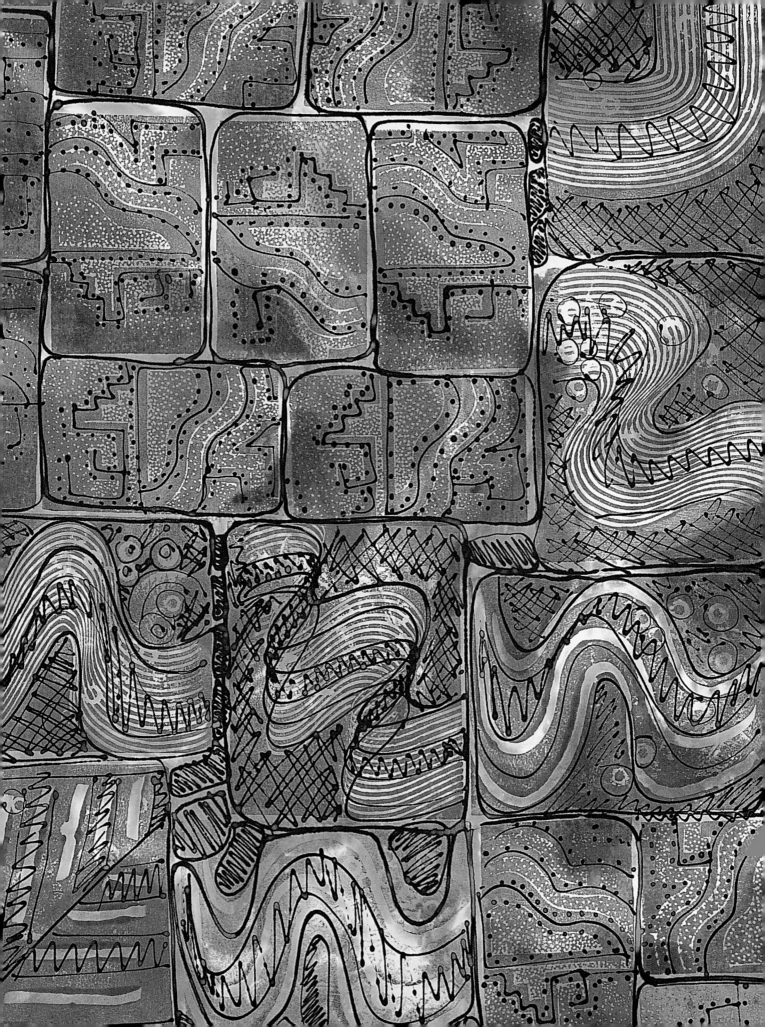

❖ ❖ ❖

References

DESIGN

Arnheim, Rudolf. *Art and Visual Perception*. Berkeley, CA: University of California Press, 1954.

Bates, Kenneth F. *Basic Design: Principles and Practices*. New York: Barnes and Noble Books, 1979.

Bayles, David, and Ted Orland. *Art and Fear*. Santa Barbara: Capra Press, 1993.

Birren, Faber. *Creative Color*. New York: Van Nostrand Reinhold, 1961.

Bothwell, Dorr, and Marlys Frey. *Notan, The Dark-Light Principle of Design*. New York: Van Nostrand Reinhold, 1968.

Bevlin, M. E. *Design Through Discovery*. New York: Holt, Rinehart and Winston, 1977.

Collier, Graham. *Form, Space and Vision*. Englewood Cliffs, NJ: Prentice-Hall, 1967.

Constantine, Mildred. *Beyond Craft: The Art Fabric*. New York: Kodansha International, 1973.

Cizikszentmihalyi, Mihaly. *Creativity*. New York: Harper Collins, 1996.

De Sausmarez, Maurice. *Basic Design: The Dynamics of Visual Form*. New York: Reinhold Publishing Corporation, 1964.

Dow, Arthur. *Composition: A Series of Exercises in Art Structure*. New York: Doubleday, 1913.

Gardner, Howard. *Art, Mind, and Brain*. New York: Basic Books, 1982.

Hargartti, Istvan, and Magdolna Hargartti. *Symmetry*. California: Shelter Publications, 1994.

Heim, Judy, and Gloria Hansen. *The Quilter's Computer Companion*. San Francisco: No Starch Press, 1997.

Herman, Lloyd E. *The Woven and Graphic Art of Anni Albers*. Washington, DC: Smithsonian Institution Press, 1985.

Itten, Johannes. *Design and Form*. New York: Van Nostrand Reinhold, 1976.

————. *The Elements of Color*. New York: Van Nostrand Reinhold, 1970.

Jung, Carl G. *The Spirit in Man, Art and Literature*. New York, Pantheon Books, 1966.

Kepes, Gyorgy. *Language of Vision*. Chicago: Paul Theobald, 1951.

Klee, Paul. *Pedagogical Sketchbook*. New York: Frederick A. Praeger, 1953.

Lauer, David. *Design Basics*. New York: Harcourt Brace Jovanovich College Publishers, 1990.

McKim, Robert H. *Thinking Visually*. New York: Van Nostrand Reinhold, 1980.

Newman, Rochelle, and Martha Boles. *Universal Patterns*. Bradford, MA: Pythagorean Press, 1992.

Pye, David. *The Nature of Design*. New York: Reinhold Publishing Corp, 1967.

Richardson, John Adkins, Floyd W. Coleman, and Michael J. Smith. *Basic Design: Systems, Elements, Applications*. Englewood Cliffs: Prentice-Hall, 1984.

Reiss, Marjorie, and Albert Schweizer. *You Can Design*. New York: McGraw Hill Book Company, 1939.

Smeets, Rene. *Signs, Symbols and Ornament*. New York: Van Nostrand Reinhold, 1975.

Wahlman, Maude Southwell. *Signs and Symbols*. New York: Museum of American Folk Art, 1993.

Washburn, Dorothy. *Symmetries of Culture*. Seattle: University of Washington Press, 1988.

Wong, Wucius. *Principles of Color Design*. New York: Van Nostrand Reinhold, 1987.

QUILTS

Colvin, Joan. *The Nature of Design*. Bothel, WA: Fiber Studio Press, 1996.

Crow, Nancy. *Quilt and Influences*. Paducah, KY: American Quilter's Society, 1990.

———. *Improvisational Quilts*. Concord, CA: C & T Publishing, 1996.

Cuzick, Dawn, ed. *Contempraory Quilts*. Asheville, NC: Lark Books, 1997.

———. *Quilt National: Contemporary Designs in Fabric*. Asheville, NC: Lark Books, 1995.

Dales, Judy B. *Curves in Motion*. Concord, CA: C & T Publishing, 1998.

Hughes, Robert. *Amish: The Art of the Quilt*. New York: Alfred A. Knopf, 1993.

James, Michael. *The Second Quiltmaker's Handbook*. Englewood Cliffs: Prentice Hall, 1981.

Leon, Eli. *Who'd A Thought It*. San Francisco: San Francisco Folk Art Museum, 1987.

Mattera, Joanne, ed. *The Quilter's Art*. Asheville, NC: Lark Books, 1981.

McDowell, Ruth B. *Art and Inspirations*. Concord, CA: C & T Publishing, 1996.

McMorris, Penny, and Michael Kile. *The Art Quilt*. San Francisco: The Quilt Digest Press, 1986.

Roe, Nancy, ed. *Fiber Expressions: The Contenporary Quilt*. Exton, PA: Schiffer Publishing Ltd., 1987.

———. *New Quilts: Interpretations and Innovations*. Exton, PA: Schiffer Publishing Ltd., 1989.

Roe, Nancy, and Holly Panich, eds. *Quilts: The State of an Art*. Exton, PA: Schiffer Publishing Ltd., 1985.

Roe, Nancy, ed. *The Quilt: New Directions for an American Tradition*. Exton, PA: Schiffer Publishing Ltd., 1983.

Shaw Robert, *The Art Quilt*. Hugh Lauter Levin Associates, Inc., 1997.

Speckman, Doreen. *Pattern Play*. Concord, CA: C & T Publishing, 1994.

Timmons, Christine. *The New Quilt 1*. Newtown, CT: Taunton Press, 1991.

———. *The New Quilt 2*. Newtown, CT: Taunton Press, 1993.

Walker, Michele. *The Passionate Quilter*. N. Pomfret, Vermont: Trafalgar Square Publishing, 1971.

SURFACE DESIGN

Dunnewold, Jane. *Complex Cloth*. Bothel, WA: Fiber Studio Press, 1996.

Heim, Judy, and Gloria Hansen. *The Quilter's Computer Companion*. San Francisco: No Starch Press, 1997.

Johnston, Ann. *Dye Painting!* Paducah, KY: American Quilter's Society, 1992.

———. *Color by Accident: Low-water Immersion Dyeing*. Lake Oswego, OR: Ann Johnston, Publisher, 1997.

Laury, Jean Ray. *Imagery on Fabric*. Concord, CA: C & T Publishing, 1997.

Noble, Elin. *Dyes and Paints*. Bothel, WA: Fiber Studio Press, 1998.

Scherer, Deidre. *Work in Fabric and Thread*. Concord, CA: C & T Publishing, 1998.

Westphal, Katherine. *The Surface Designer's Art*. Ashville, NC: Lark Books, 1993.

❖ ❖ ❖

Index

Page numbers referring to images of quilts or quilt details are bold and italic; those referring to images of swatches of fabrics or groups of thread are bold.